# Make a Million in your PJ's

**Tracey Leak**

Cover design: Alvin T. Cruz & Adi Bustaman
Photograhy (front cover): Ben Robinson
Tracey's photo (back cover): Nick McAlinden, Imago Photography

# www.TheArtOfHomeBasedBusiness.com

# With Thanks....

This book has been a journey and no journey goes without help along the way, so I'd like to take a moment to acknowledge and thank those who helped me.

Firstly, I want to thank my interviewees – Joel, Stephen, Annette, Craig, Paul, Amy, Michael and Chris. They were not only humble and open to questions, they were gracious with their time, energy and information. All took extra time to chat, help me and share their wisdom. Contacting each of them took me out of my comfort zone (some out of my time zone!) and after meeting them, I was amazed not only by their knowledge, but also by the fact that they were just such normal, nice people.

I want to thank Mum, Dad, Kim & Craig. As corny as it may sound, my family always believed in me and on this journey they shared my excitement. While others questioned what I was doing, they just told me to go for it. I am so grateful that you are my family and that you continue to encourage me, support me and always back me – no matter how crazy my ideas may sound. Special thanks to my sister-in-law Deb for her great ideas shared in our discussions.

Everyone has great friends that help them along the way. My friends who should never go without mention are Kate and Kent. Kate started as my business coach, she is my business partner, she was once even my boss, but now more than anything else, she is my friend. Kate comes as a package with her husband Kent, who allows me to do crazy business things with Kate, but has also been one of my greatest coaches in life. Kate and Kent have always looked out for me. Without Kate's assistance, especially in my early years of business, I would not be the person I am today. I would never have ventured out of my comfort zone to find the life I had always dreamed of or decided that I could pick up the phone and ask someone I wanted to learn from if they would give me an hour of their time.

Finally, a thank you to you. I hope that you read this book and really learn and understand how you too can make your home-based business a success.

To access your **FREE** videos of these interviews, please go to:

## www.TheArtOfHomeBasedBusiness.com/interviews

(Access Code: pjmillions)

## *Look for ways to add value . . .*

Tracey Leak grew up in country Australia in a home-based business. She started her first business when she was just seven years old.

Tracey lived in Canada for a year on a Rotary Youth Exchange, returning to Australia to complete high school before completing a Bachelor of Applied Science at the Royal Melbourne Institute of Technology.

Working as a radiographer, Tracey was unable to ignore the entrepreneur in her heart. After being diagnosed with a brain tumour, which she no longer has, she made her leap into being a full-time small business owner.

Tracey's journey led her to become a business coach after much coaxing from her own business coach. Seven years after helping many business owners find their success, Tracey has returned to her childhood roots as a specialist in home-based business.

Tracey still works from home in Brisbane, Australia and can be found most days in her PJ's.

**Check out Tracey's blog, <u>FREE</u> webinar & download your <u>FREE</u> e-book (Which Home-Based Business?)**

**www.TheArtOfHomeBasedBusiness.com**

# *Contents:*

# Introduction

A very good friend of mine once said 'You need to have a mentor'. Mentors can be someone you know, or would like to know, and the easiest way to find a great mentor is to read a book. This book has been created to bring you not just one mentor, but eight, and each of the eight has been interviewed to share with you the philosophy behind his or her success.

Before jumping into the interviews, I'd love to share with you my journey of writing this book. Not to prove something or gain recognition for what I've achieved, but because I want you to realise that you can go after the things you want and achieve what may seem to be beyond your wildest dreams.

I grew up in a family with a home-based business. My Mum and Dad were entrepreneurs before I was born. This foundation has allowed me to take risks in business when my intuition gives me a gut feeling to 'go for it'.

My parents worked hard all of their lives. We lived in a country town in Western Victoria in Australia. When I say country town I mean a population of one hundred, with no shops. My primary school had about twenty kids— in total. We were okay financially, but never wealthy. I know now that they had money issues and cash flow challenges, as does every business owner, but I never knew about them when I growing up.

Mum and Dad worked hard to help my sister, brother and I realise that there was a great big world out there. When I was seventeen, I was chosen to go on a year long Rotary Youth Exchange to Canada. What a life-changing experience it was to live in another country and stand on my own two feet in the world.

I won't bore you with the full details, but after high school and university I worked as a radiographer, you know, taking X-rays. I grew to hate it and my inner entrepreneur surfaced.

When I was twenty-seven, I was diagnosed with a brain tumour. It was the best thing to ever happen to me. It woke me up, taught me to start living my life and to stop operating on autopilot.

I read a book *Billionaire in Training*, about business and acquiring a business with no money down. That's how I got my first business, a hair salon. I took over the lease and I discovered I had a lot to learn.

I was referred to my business coach, Kate, by my brother. Kate helped me become the person I am today by always asking me a better question and helping me see the truth—which I didn't always like. Through Kate's guidance in my businesses she got to know me and finally encouraged me to join her and become a business coach myself.

Mentors can come to you by choice, others appear as if by divine intervention. Joel Comm (yes, one of my interviewees) came by divine intervention. I was attending a seminar with about a dozen different speakers. I almost didn't go, but it was free so I decided I could always leave at any time. The third speaker on the first day was Joel. Among lots of fantastic content, he asked us to write down what it was that we were passionate about. I had three things on my list: business, kids, and helping people. He then asked us to think about a niche from one of those things we had written. I realised at that moment what I loved to do. I loved to help people in business, in their home-based business. Why? Because it combined all of my passions and I loved working from home personally. That seminar sparked my excitement.

Have you ever been on the internet and from an initial search, you end up somewhere totally different just by following links? That is how I came to this book.

I had so loved what Joel spoke about that I googled him. I watched his YouTube videos, I purchased his *Elevate* DVD series and watched his reality internet show, *The Next Internet Millionaire*. It was in these videos that I discovered the idea of writing a book.

I have always dreamed of writing books, even though my high school English teacher told me that I wasn't any good in the subject.

Only the day before someone had said to me, 'Sometimes you have to go out on a limb because that is where the fruit is.' So I went out on a limb.

This was the beginning of a new chapter (excuse the pun) in my life and what an amazing chapter it has become.

I went from excitement—basically jumping off the walls—to immense fear and panic that this was happening way too easily and I must either be dreaming, or there was a big catch.

So how do you turn an idea into an end product? By the way, the ending of this story is a happy one because you are reading the finished product!

As my book was all about who I was going to interview, I searched to find people who I really wanted to meet and whose wisdom I wanted to hear. I got lucky some would say, but my belief is that if you are true to yourself and on your path—if you turn up—so will the people to help you.

Kate (my coach) has often said that everyone needs to find a mentor and when you find one, you should ask him or her to lunch. This is a great piece of advice, but now I was going to do it for real. Not only did I want to meet the people I chose, but I wanted to interview them too. Plus all but one of them were in the USA.

The number one question I have been asked on this journey is, 'Was it hard to get the interviews?' For me it was really easy. I picked up the phone and called them. Some I emailed, others I organised meetings with them through their assistants. They all shared one thing in common, they were all normal people who wanted to help me.

After doing one interview in Australia, I jumped on a plane to do seven interviews in six cities in ten days in the USA. Two of those days were spent on a plane flying to and from the USA. It was crazy, it was fun, it was living my dream—it was living my *life*. For me personally, it was life-changing. I was filled with great knowledge and advice that I will soon share with you.

How do you feel when your wildest dreams are coming true?

I see-sawed between excitement, determination, joy, and pure belief in what I was doing to: *What am I thinking? Who do I think I am? Am I kidding myself that I can do this?*

How did I go on?

Everything is about association. This is why mentors are so helpful in an entrepreneurial journey. Who are you listening to?

Every time I felt doubt or strayed off the path, I came back to these interviews you are about to read. They gave me the wisdom I needed, they gave me the feeling of being on track. I owe it to you to deliver their wisdom, that has helped me so much.

My Mum, Dad, Kim, Craig, Kate and Kent were the people who helped me beat my self-doubt. 'Stop listening to yourself and start talking to yourself,' were the words of a great mentor of mine. When I could only listen to myself, these people helped me see that I was still on track and that with a pure heart, my dream would ignite the flames of the dreams of others.

That is why I am sharing my story with you. I may not have it all together, but every day I keep living my life, going after my dreams and not listening to those destructive thoughts. I tackle every obstacle that is on my path. I just keep going and choose not to quit.

My Dad used to say to me that he never cared if I won or if I got an 'A', he only wanted to know, 'Did I do my best?' Because if I had done my best, he could ask for no more.

So as I prepare for my next journey, developing and delivering information to help other home based business owners like me go for their dreams, I will remember my Dad's words and always do my best.

My goal is to serve you and I certainly hope that you discover for yourself the wisdom on the pages to follow that will help you in your business, and in your life, as much as they have helped me.

Read my interviews with the millionaire entrepreneurs. They have different backgrounds, different journeys and different points of view. I'm sure you will find the ones who resonate with you, which will most likely be different than those chosen by the next person who reads them. Read, learn and implement these thoughts, ideas, and lessons.

Enjoy and be inspired.

*Tracy*

*Introducing . . .*

# Joel Comm

I was so nervous! How do you meet, let alone interview a person who has completely changed your life? I think all of us have a need for others to like us and I wanted Joel to like me and think that what I was setting out to achieve was a good thing.

Joel came to Australia and spoke at a seminar I attended. His presentation blew me away. In that presentation he just gave and gave and then gave more information.

What he was saying really resonated with me. So many people are looking to make money doing business in the world of the internet. Joel challenged us to find what we were passionate about, give great content and add value. Then, and only then, look at ways to 'monetize' that. It was in his seminar that I wrote down that I was passionate about home-based business.

In the weeks that followed, I read and watched everything to do with Joel Comm. This lead me to develop my business as it is today, including this book. It seemed only right that I interview Joel to share his views. I am sure they will help you as much as they helped me. Enjoy this interview, but more importantly, learn – it could change your life as well.

## *The interview with Joel Comm . . .*

**Tracey:** What I'd love to do is just start with you just telling us your story of how you got started. It's an incredible story.

**Joel:** I've always been into computers. I had a TRS80 Model 1 computer in 1979. That was the first truly affordable, personal computer and I remember my mother saying to me when I spent money on it (at fourteen I was working at a pizza place and I was saving money), 'What are you going to do with a computer?' Well that was all fun and games. Who really knew? But I just knew there was this attraction to them.

I was calling into bulletin board systems—that was the version of the internet back then—it was like these mini nets at 300 bps. Just slow. That was 1979, so technically I've been online for over thirty years, which when you think that the web's only been around sixteen, that's a long time.

Fast forward to 1994 and I'm working as an encyclopedia salesman, selling Britannica's and doing well. Learned a lot about sales from Zig Zigler, this fantastic motivator and salesman.

I was also a mobile DJ. I already had the entrepreneur blood running through me. I was a DJ in college on a radio station and I realised you can make $100, $125 an hour DJ'ing wedding receptions and pool parties and this type of thing.

So I had that entrepreneurial thing going. I've always been a computer gamer. I love computer games. Still to this day, I play games on my computer. It's a great way to blow off steam. I remember reading a computer game magazine and thinking, I bet the guys who write these articles get all the free software they want.

Well, being married with two kids, one here and one on the way, I thought, 'You can't afford to buy a lot of software, so what if I started my own little software review rag?' And I did. I created the *Dallas Fort Worth Software Review*.

I had software companies sending me software all the time, all this free software, but I couldn't afford to pay writers. So I put ads on what was then America Online, in Prodigy, in bulletin board services saying, 'Looking for writers for a software review magazine. I can't pay you, but you'll get to keep the software you review.' So it was kind of like a joint venture, my successful barter. I had forty people sign up to write reviews for me. So I did this little software review magazine.

In 1995, I got introduced to the World Wide Web and turned my little magazine into a website called worldvillage.com. I've got an approach to software reviews that a lot of the other online sites don't have. I'm very much into family and creating wholesome content that I believe I would want my children to interact with. So we reviewed software from a family-friendly perspective. We added chat rooms that were clean and monitored and moderated and games that people could play online.

I was on the web and thought I would make a ton and we went through money fast. Nothing was as easy as it seems, but you have to persist and my faith plays a huge role in who I am and in my success. I don't really take credit for my success. My faith in God is really what drives me and while I could say, 'Oh look at this cool thing I did here', I can point to all of the really important things that have happened in my business and say that wasn't me, that was a God thing. Some people would call it the universe, I beg to differ, it's more personal than that for me.

We were down to like eighty-seven cents in our checking account. My wife remembers this clearly. I say it was a dollar eighty-seven, she says it was eighty-seven cents, so she's right. She remembers, I don't remember.

That was in 1996 and I just began praying. I said, 'All right, I thought this was what I was supposed to do.' I quit my job. I felt like this was where I was being led. And I just said 'All right God, if you want me to continue with this, you're going to have to drop the money out of the sky.'

That week—within a week—I got an email from a gentleman in Seattle. I'm in Texas at the time. This man from Seattle, Washington, who I had never heard of, was representing a Japanese media conglomerate that I had never heard of. He said that they were interested in licensing the content that I have in worldvillage.com, translating it and locating it onto a Japanese site. I'm on the phone with him and fortunately, one thing I learned is always keep your mouth shut.

You know, it's better to listen than to talk, it's why God gave us two ears and one mouth. I figure they're going to offer me a couple of hundred bucks or something to do this. He said, 'They'd like to pay you five thousand dollars a month.' I'm on the other end of the phone going, 'Okay.' Turned out to be seventy-five hundred dollars a month for a three-year contract for what would take me approximately three to four hours a month to fulfil. Call it what you want, I call it an answer to prayer and what was necessary to facilitate the on-going operations of my business and not only that, but the *prosperity* of the business, because that was a lot of money then—still is a lot of money, but it was great.

The business continued and in 1997, I received an email from my webmaster, who knew I was into playing games and he said, 'Hey, check out this site this kid made—springerspan.com, named after the guy's Springer Spaniel.' It was one of the web's first multi-player game sites where you could play hearts, spades, chess, checkers, bridge and backgammon against other people in real time and nobody was using it.

He had three or four of his friends testing it, kicking the tires and so I wrote him an email and I said, 'Hey, I've got this website. We've got thousands of people coming each month. What if we partnered up on this and grew this game site into something really cool?' After negotiating, he said yes and so we rebranded it classicgames.com, which I thought was a much better name than springerspan.com, although he fought me on it.

I began promoting and marketing it, and we put thousands of people into it. I think at our peak we had about six hundred people at one time playing it, which was a far shout from his three or four friends. I tried to market it out there and the portals, they weren't paying attention at that time, they were thinking that it was all just 'Search'. But one company was doing more than Search for their portal and that was Yahoo!

They were very visionary and they came knocking on the virtual door—they sent me an email. Eric Schwartz, at the Yahoo! games development, Yahoo Entertainment, said, 'We're looking at making a games portion of our portal and we'd like to talk about partnering with you. Long story short, they ended up acquiring classicgames.com which became Yahoo! Games.

To this day, if you look at the avatars that you can choose from, one of them is a guy with a cap, glasses and a goatee—and at that time I had a goatee—so I've got a little effigy of me in Yahoo! games. That was a seven-figure deal, so it was really great.

At that point, I was able to get out of debt completely, pay off the house, pay off the cars and just not owe anyone and put some money away, because you never know. A lot of people come into a windfall and they go spend it all. Stuff never fills your needs, it's just stuff. People find that out after they have too much stuff. So we put some away. We had more than enough for what our needs were. And then I rode the boom.

The internet, that first wave, was tremendous. It was crazy money. Crazy. I had a site called dealofday.com, still do. It's ten years old right now. It was a shopper's paradise. We would list all of the various coupons and deals that merchants would put online.

Now, again, if you look at the history of the things I've done, I've been passionate about every one of them. Creating software reviews because I'm passionate about playing games and reviewing them from a healthy perspective. Building a game site because I'm into games and turning that passion into profits. I'm into online shopping and saving money. I love using coupons. Why did I create my own site? To help others do that.

All the successes that I've had have come from that place deep within me that says, 'I'm excited about this.' It really perplexes me when people say, 'What are hot niches?', 'What should I get into that would be profitable?', because I think it's backwards.

You heard me speak in Brisbane, that's my goal. Yes, I want to teach, but I want to inspire people first. Inspire, educate, entertain—in that order. Because if you can't light a fire under people, then they're not going to be able to do anything with the material. If you can't make them laugh a little bit along the way, then they won't be able to digest it as easily. So, kind of, what you see is what you get. Even as you're talking to me now, you'll see it's no different here than on the stage. I'm no different at home, I'm the same person, there's a consistency because I don't want to play-act. I want to be real. I encourage other people to be real as well. You can spot a phony a mile away.

Then in 2000, everything flew apart. Because we had businesses that weren't based on real business models that were sustainable and could be profitable, it was inevitable that things were going to fall apart. But I knew, and I knew that I knew, and I knew that I knew that I knew that I knew, that it would come back again and I told my wife.

For years we lived off savings. I had to lay off everybody, including myself. I stopped paying myself a salary, but I wanted to keep the websites going because I knew it was going to come back. I didn't know how, I didn't know when, but I knew we could survive and make it through.

And in 2004, Google came out with their AdSense program for publishers. I tried it and I failed miserably at it. I let it go for nine months. And nine months later, April 2005, I was sitting in a conference room, in a small conference mastermind of maybe twenty to thirty people. The guy sitting next to me, a friend of mine, had his laptop open and he had his AdSense report up on the screen. I looked at it and I saw that he was making two hundred to three hundred dollars a day and I thought, 'What am I doing wrong?'

That day, sitting in that conference room, I began testing page placement with my AdSense blocks. I began testing colour schemes, block sizes, etc.

On the previous day I had made about twenty-three dollars with AdSense. That day I made over eighty dollars. I even told them in that room. I said, 'Guys, you're not going to believe this, but my revenue just went up like this with making a few simple changes.' So I kept testing it. I kept making changes and my revenue went up, up, up. Pretty soon I'm making over five hundred dollars a day and I've got some of my associates saying, 'What are you doing?'

So I start sharing with them some of the strategies. After a bit they said, 'People would probably pay for this type of information.' *Duh!* Okay, I'm a little thick. I've never really been in the information marketing niche. There are people that have gone before me: Yanik Silver, Mark Joyner, Paul Myers. There are a lot of legends on internet marketing, but I never entered into that arena. I wasn't really even all that aware of it. I was busy creating content sites and developing other products. So I thought, 'Okay, how do I do an e-book?'

I wrote a sixty-six page e-book called, *What Google Never Told You About Making Money with AdSense* and it had a lot of the strategies that I used to bump up my AdSense income. I thought if I can make ten thousand dollars with this in a year that would be aces. So I put it out there and put it into ClickBank and a shopping cart service and offered an affiliate program where I paid commission on it.

An affiliate by the name of Paul Myers, that I had known from a Mastermind group shared it with his list. Orders started coming in. Other people that were on his list that were marketers saw it and thought, 'Can I affiliate and promote this to my list?' and so it began to take on this snowball effect. We sold ten thousand dollars worth of e-books in the first week. *The first week!* I'm like, 'This is crazy, this is insane, this is great!' I kind of sat back and enjoyed it and began to learn who some of the people were in the industry.

It was the end of January 2005 that the e-book came out. Then that summer I released a second, updated edition which sold for ninety-seven dollars. It went from sixty-seven dollars to seventy-seven dollars to ninety-seven dollars. It was twice the size, had a lot more content, and it sold even more—just sold like crazy. In October of that year, Jeff Walker, who's known for the Product Lunch Formula and is big in internet marketing, was a friend of mine and Jeff suggested that I go to a seminar in LA by a fellow called Armand Morin - Armand Morin's Big Seminar. He said, 'I think it would be good for you.'

Why listen to people talk? I didn't even realise that they sell from the stage, I just didn't even think about it because I didn't know what to expect. I signed up and I paid two thousand dollars to go to it. Two thousand dollars—that's a lot of money, that was the perspective.

I try to wake people to how unproductive and how unhealthy that perspective is when you're trying to grow a business. I didn't have a business perspective. I was looking at money, not thinking of the big picture. Travel costs, hotel costs, time away from home. I almost didn't go.

My wife said, 'You need to go.' I said, 'Why?' She said, 'I don't know, you just need to go.' Well, it's taken me years and years of marriage, but I've learned to listen to my wife. Her intuition is just superior. She's like a radar, *beep*, *beep*, *beep*. If she says it, I better pay attention.

I went. I showed up at the hotel Thursday night (the conference was to start Friday) and as I'm walking through the halls there was a bunch of people over by the bar and they're waving, 'Joel'. What? It's like someone here knows me. There's Armand Morin, he's waving me over. I've never even met the guy. Here's Armand, he's this big time marketer, it's his conference. Whoa. I thought, *Cool*.

Then there are these other marketers, Craig Parian and Dr Michael Ming and Gary Ambrose and these guys know who I am. They recognised my picture, maybe from an email from me. People that are attending are whispering, I hear them when I go in the hallway, 'That's Joel Comm.' I'm like, *What?* I didn't realise that I already had this minor celebrity status because of the success of the e-book.

As I said, I went to the conference. I still wasn't exactly sure why I was there. The first speaker was Stephen Pearce and he got up on stage and he just had everybody paying attention. There had to be four hundred or five hundred people there and everybody's just enraptured and listening to him and he's killing it and I think to myself, I could do that. I want to do that. The thought of getting up and speaking in front of people scared me to death. My wife had always told me that that was a gift that I had. Didn't matter, still scared me to death. But I knew I could be on that stage. I can teach people, I can sell product.

I locked that away and left that conference. In March of 2006, I came out with a third edition of my AdSense e-book and I also came out with a physical copy of my AdSense book called *The AdSense Code*, published in Morgan James Publishing. I met David Hancock at that big seminar and that change my life too, because he explained how you could sell thousands of copies of your e-book at ninety-seven dollars, but when you've got a physical book it raises your credibility. Just automatically, there's something about that physical book. And so I got the book done with him and it came out in March 2006.

That month I also went to Yanik Silver's Underground Internet Marketing event. Wasn't speaking, just went to it. There was a gentleman there, a long, blonde hair, hippie-type, young guy, by the name of Eric Holmlund. Eric was passing out flyers that said JP with Eric. He came up to me and said, 'Hey, I've wanted to meet you. I believe from what I've read about you that we share a similar faith. If I ever come up with an idea to help you in your business, can I contact you?' I said, 'Sure.'

A few weeks later, Eric sent me an email. It says, 'I've got an idea.' You've got thousands of people who are your AdSense customers and they're making this money with AdSense, or they want to, but a lot of them don't have a website. What if we created a product that would allow them to get a website  up and running easily, that was optimised for AdSense placement. We call it Instant AdSense Templates.' He says, 'I'll do your work, you put your teaching and your brand on it and we launch it together.'

That summer, that July, we launched Instant AdSense Templates and we sold three hundred thousand dollars worth of product in one week. It was just like, 'Wow! This whole information product thing is great.' If you create product that meets a need and brings value, people will pay for it.

Of course by then I had really begun to dominate the AdSense space. I now had a physical book. I was known. People could come along and say they're the AdSense experts, but you can say it all day long once you've got branding. I tried to brand myself even further. People started calling me Dr AdSense, which I thought was really amusing. Do you know where it came from? I started signing my emails *Dr AdSense* so I would show up somewhere and hear, 'Hey, Dr AdSense!' Looking back it was a stupid name and I stopped using it. But the point was I branded myself and when you do that people will start using it, if it makes sense to them. Hey, everybody thinks he's Dr AdSense now.

It's kind of funny. We did Instant AdSense Templates and then what we realized was that's what Mark Joyner teaches. Mark is my friend. He's got a place in New Zealand and America and is a popular internet marketer. Mark says, 'Find a thirsty audience, sell them a glass of water and then sell them a second glass.' In other words, if they're thirsty and they like what they got the first time around, they're going to want more. So with the second edition of Instant AdSense Templates we launched in October 2006, we created the product, an up-sell and a continuity program, so that people could buy more of what we had.

We did over a million dollars in product sales in five days on a low price point product. I mean it's not uncommon to hear of a million-dollar launch now, but of a $297 or $197 product? We sold a lot— something like thirty-eight hundred units in five days. It was tremendous. We had the continuity built into it so people could keep getting more each month.

After that I talked to Eric and I said, 'What do you want to do next?' and he says, 'I want to get into video.' So after I moved to Colorado in February 2007, I was in the shower, which is where, I don't know why, but some of my best ideas come from. (Not sure if it's being idle, just letting your brain think, or the water pounding on your skull, stimulating synapses to fire—I don't know what it is).

I'm a reality TV fan, I confess. I watch *Survivor* and I used to watch *The Apprentice* too. I enjoy that type of drama and I thought video's getting really big online. What if we combined reality TV with an Internet-based show, but raised the bar for production value. I called Eric about it and I said, 'You've been wanting to get in video. What do you think of producing this show?' And he said, 'All right, let's do it.' We called it *The Next Internet Millionaire*.

By spring of that year, we put out a casting call for people. They were to audition on YouTube. We got close to three hundred people to make a video to say, from all over the world, why they wanted to be a contestant on the show. We narrowed it down to fifty with some voting and some selection and then we picked twelve people, six men, six women, most Americans, two Canadians, one from the UK, and a gentleman from Costa Rica.

We flew them all here to Colorado. We rented a warehouse, turned it into a set for two weeks and put them through the learning process. We brought in some of the biggest names in internet marketing to teach them. Armand Morin, Mark Joyner, Jeff Walker, Rich Schefren, Perry Marshall.

There were twelve of them and we put them to the test through both group and individual challenges. We eliminated people and at the end there was one person left standing who won the title, "The Next Internet Millionaire". They got to do a joint venture with me, in which we grossed seventy grand in one week and they also got twenty-five thousand dollars cash. It was the first of its kind. Nobody's done anything of its equal online, just for the internet. If you go to www.nextinternetmillionaire.com, you can watch it. We've also got a DVD box that you can buy on Amazon.com, which is the whole show.

What you see here is a pattern. I like to do things that nobody's done before and part of it is out of necessity, because I get bored just repeating what someone else has done. Why not be creative and come up with new stuff? If there is something that's been done that can be done better and I'm excited about it, I'm all up for that too. I'm into creating quality product that actually makes a difference.

So in doing *The Next Internet Millionaire*, I realised from the successful marketers that came onto the set to help teach the contestants, that everybody's got a story, just like you're hearing my story right now. Armand Morin used to sell vacuum cleaners. Mike Filsaime sold cars. John Reece was over one hundred thousand dollars in the hole before he became known as a brilliant internet marketer. So I thought what about a book that would trace the history of internet marketing.

Because I'd read books on eBay and Amazon and Google—all the big companies—but what about the big underground movement that's regular people? And so *Click Here to Order* was born. I did over fifty hours of interviews to get people's stories and compile them into this biography, which was designed to inspire people.

If a former DJ and encyclopedia salesman can follow his passion and find successes online, why not you? I'm not that special. I'm not that smart. I'm really not. I got average grades in school. I barely graduated in college because I spent my time partying my way through. I like to play video games.

So what makes me so special? Well, other than just being special because I'm an individual and I'm alive, there's nothing. It's all down to people who will follow their passion and take action.

Just like you're doing, which is why I'm sure this book is going to be a huge success for you. Because you're following your heart and your passion. I'm excited to see that happen for you.

*Click Here to Order* came out, and around that time, Apple announced that they were going to be making a developer program so people could create applications for the iPhone. I'm a huge iPhone fan and instantly we knew here that we wanted to do that as well. We found a developer and brought him on staff.

We developed a number of applications: iVote, shopping coupons that related to our Deal of the Day website, but the most infamous of the applications is the iFart.

iFarts appeared all over the media. Bill Marr talked about us on his HBO show, David Duchovny used it on the set of a movie he was filming. I was on the *Daily Show* with John Stewart, which you can Google that to see the clip. Cathy Lee Gifford used it on the *Today Show* and she and Hoda played the Dirty Raoul.

**Tracey:** It must have been a funny day when you came up with it!

**Joel:** It was. We all laughed because we had all kinds of ideas that we put on the whiteboard. You put a bunch of guys in the room—and we knew.

Of course, we added features to it that were fun as well, it wasn't just sounds. We added a stylish look to it so it wasn't just another iPhone app.

We shot up to number one in just a matter of days. And we were at number one for twenty-two days straight and got written about all over the place, including the *New York Times Magazine*.

They even did a full article on the access of an application like iFart and it was called 'Dumb and Dumber 2.0'. It was all about the silly things that people spend money on. To this day, when people make reference to dumb apps that people spend money on that have been successful for the iPhone, iFart is the de facto standard.

We've gone down in Apple history as being that, and it still sells a few hundred units each day. People still enjoy it. Over half a million units sold. We do create other apps as well. In fact, we're working on one as of today that we feel has the potential to go to number one as well with a totally different type of appeal. I'll say it's in the gaming sector, but that's as far as I'll mention right now.

What else have I done? Oh, couple of other things. Around 2008, I looked at some of the literature that had been out there in internet marketing and newsletters. The physical material was not of a real top-quality nature and if people are going to be paying monthly fees for a subscription, we want to make sure we bring value. So we created the *Top One Report*. This is a full-colour, twenty-four page publication. It's beautifully done and not only has it got a pretty face, but the content in it is top notch—from me and my team and very select guest authors.

So anybody that wants a copy of this, we'll give them a copy for a dollar. You just go to toponereport.com, and then if you want to continue receiving it it's just $29.95 a month. So the newsletter's been going for over a year. *[This report is now available online FREE]*

Last October, we put on a seminar here in Denver. It was an expensive seminar. We wanted to keep it small on purpose. People came and we filmed the whole thing and now it's actually a complete DVD set called *The Elevate Blueprint*, which you yourself have. Have you watched it all?

**Tracey:** I've watched it all.

**Joel:** And probably learned a ton.

**Tracey:** Yes - I watched it straight over two days.

**Joel:** Beautiful ...

**Tracey:** I have to say, I love it's packaging, like the *Top One Report*, all-colour printed. It's top quality.

**Joel:** Because I wanted to reflect the quality of what's inside. That we believe that this content is so strong that to present it, you know, CDs with home-printed labels or just a plain box or sleeves, is doing it a disservice. It needs to look like it really is quality and this is now. It starts at $997. There are up-sells so that you can get more with it and some conferences, up to two thousand dollars because of all the bonuses that we include.

**Tracey:** That was an awesome seminar.

**Joel:** Thank you. You know it's amazing how you just fall into things. In May 2007, I got into social media, well Twitter in particular. Didn't get it for six months—kind of left it sitting.

In December of 2007, I really started using Twitter and interacting with people. I wrote a report that I put out on how to use Twitter for business. Mark Joyner said that he was looking for somebody to write a book on doing Twitter for business and we got on the phone. The end result is this book, *Twitter Power*, with the foreword by none other than Anthony Robbins. The book came out in February of 2009 and has been in the *BookScan* Top 50 ever since and continues to sell great.

It's now opened me up, branding me as a 'social media expert'—everybody uses that terminology and it really kind of makes me crazy. So I prefer to call myself a 'social media evangelist'.

To rewind a little bit, I told you I knew I wanted to speak on platforms, but I was scared of it. In 2006, I began to get invitations for small venues. Today I speak on Tony Robbins' stage, Harv Eker's stage and Chris Howard's stage. I travel around the world and say no to events way more often than I say yes.

It's an incredible blessing for me, because you can tell when I'm on stage that I am loving what I'm doing and there is nowhere that I am more in my element than in front of people, attempting to communicate and inspire them and give them very practical things that they can do to build their own business online.

I talk about how some of this stuff is so easy even my mother could do it and she does. www.travelswithsheila.com is her blog and she doesn't make a ton of money, but she gets deductions. She loves what she's doing. She's into soft adventure travel and so her passion is encouraging other people to travel and see the world and do it on a budget—to show that you can do travel on a budget. So she'll take her video camera with her. She's sixty-seven years old. She travels half the year because she loves it. She doesn't want to miss any of it. So, she can do it and have a blog and put out radios and post articles. What's your excuse, right? What's your excuse why you don't have one? There's more going on, but that's my story.

**Tracey:** Are you keen to do another live seminar like *Elevate*?

**Joel:** No immediate intent, because really it's all in the DVDs. These are strategies that we use. You can apply the stuff that we teach here to any niche or any market and a lot of it you can apply even to offline businesses, because it's a philosophy. So putting on a seminar's a big deal and being in the seminar business is a tough thing. If I can't come to your town, here's how I come to your town, through my DVDs.

We're really proud of this. This is the flagship product, and anybody who wants to learn from us, they've got to have this. We priced it right, too. A lot of people price sets like this at two thousand to five thousand dollars. I thought, you know, what with things a little tougher, let's make it easy for people. So at $997, it's very reasonable.

**Tracey:** So *The AdSense Code* actually became a *New York Times* bestseller. How did that come about?

**Joel:** I don't know. We sold a lot of books in a short period of time. The whole book industry and how they report is a mystery. If there was a formula that everybody knew, then everybody would be trying to use that formula. And here's the dirty little secret. Now we didn't do this with *AdSense Code*, but we came to find out after, that a lot of the books that hit the bestseller lists, that they buy them themselves through a number of channels. Turns out, you know, the big reporting channels, Barnes & Noble, Borders, Amazon and a handful of others, they see a concentrated number of orders in a short period of time and they report those, that's how people go up the list.

So, there's been more times than we can count that books that seem to be selling a lot are really being purchased by the author or their company. So the lists, they don't mean a ton, it's nice to be able to say. But I am proud to say that we did not do that with *The AdSense Code*. It hit the *New York Times* list on its own merit. So I'm excited about that. I'm surprised *Twitter Power* hasn't yet, but we're still hopeful.

**Tracey:** So, that brings up an interesting point, not a question I had on my list, but about values and ethics in business. How do you feel about that?

**Joel:** I think they're greatly needed. You've got to have values. You know, people who come from a perspective of 'morality is relative', they haven't thought it through to its logical conclusion, because that's chaos.

If you decide for yourself what's right or wrong, then there's no standard for that. Then what's right for you might be wrong for somebody else. You say, 'well if it doesn't hurt somebody else'. Well, if you do it wrong, it's going to hurt somebody else. It's the rule of the universe. So we try our best to operate in an honest and ethical fashion, that we always seek to bring value through our offers and to market in a way that's transparent, so people can see the value.

I've made mistakes from time to time. Like, for example, we offered our *AdSense* book for people for ninety-nine dollars, the e-book, over a year ago. And as part of it, they were put into a subscription for this *Top One Report*. It was very clear on the page you get this bonus: we'll send you one issue and then it's going to be $29.95 a month. And on the order form it was there as well.

But people don't read. They don't read what they're getting. Because I want to be totally transparent and above board, our terms and conditions are always right there. You think people would know with a trial what *trial* means. Trial means you buy it, you try it, and then it converts. It's been done for centuries, right? But we give refunds and we try to have the best customer service we can.

I've got a call centre here in the building, staffed with ten people, and they're here to answer the phones. We want to make sure that people have their needs met—their expectations met and then discover what they're trying to do with their business.

Our success consultants go beyond taking orders or cancelling and refunding an order. They ask people questions about what they're passionate about and do they have a website, would they like help getting a website. We try to find the products that we have that will best serve them. Because I don't just want people's money. Anybody can make money. Can you make a difference? That's the question. That's what we try to do.

**Tracey:** There's a great story about how you came to have an office instead of working from home—involving your wife.

**Joel:**  Yeah, this was early 2000s. I had been working at home for years and my wife suggested that maybe I'd do better if I got an office out of the house and I said, 'But I like working at home.' She looked at me and she said, 'Joel, if you don't leave, I can't miss you.' Which was brilliant. I mean could you think of a more loving, wise way to make the case? After that I was like 'Oh, okay,' and it was a good thing because it allowed me to hire somebody and have a space to call my own and not be underfoot. She's raising the kids and I'm always kind of there and a little space for both of us is a good thing.

**Tracey:**  So what's some of the cool stuff you've got to do now that you've made some money?

**Joel:**  I get to travel. I'm getting ready to head to California to speak at two major events in October, which will be passed for those who see this now. I went to the UK, actually to speak at an event with over four thousand people. So I'm excited about that.
    I've got a new book idea that I'm working on right now, with just a brilliant marketing campaign attached to it. And when I say brilliant, please know that I'm not going brilliant, I'm going *brilliant*. It's like, 'Thanks for the idea. Love it. Going to do it.' We've got a mobile marketing system that we're getting ready to roll out. We've got new iPhone apps that I'm working on. New products to help people make money online, websites—a lot of stuff.

**Tracey:**  So if someone came up to you in the street and said, 'What you've done is great, but I could never do what you've done', what would you say to them?

**Joel:**  You're right, you can't do what I've done. You can only do what you can do. I believe every person has God-given talents, skills, abilities, personality, looks—you're a package. This is the package deal. Thirty pounds overweight and all. You know, this is what I am and it makes me.

I think that everybody's created for a reason with a purpose and a lot of people squander that. They never discover what that purpose is, and it's the saddest thing ever to not have lived out even a portion of why you were here. But I think as you look inwards and discover what that is and figure out what sets your heart aflame, what makes you get out of bed in the morning and pursue that thing, then you're not going to be me, you don't want to be me. Why would you want to be?

You want to do what you're called to do. Figure out what that thing is and then do it. You're not going to get excited about the same things I'm excited about. We tend to idolise people, put them on a pedestal and now that I'm in the speaker's world and instead of sitting in the audience and looking up on stage going, 'Ooh, I'm impressed', I see what it looks like from up there and I'm not impressed.

We're all just people, you know. I know people in internet marketing, in personal development, business, real estate, travel, all these different realms, and I'm not impressed by what people have accomplished. I'm impressed by their character, who they are.

Are you honest? Are you ethical? Do you have integrity? Are you giving and charitable? I know people who others think are wildly successful, but I consider them failures because of their character. I think who you are is far more important than what you've done. Now you can be both, you can be a person of integrity and, hopefully if you are, you're also doing important things and you're serving others and you're making a difference.

Seek to be who you are and not somebody else. You can model strategies and techniques after what somebody's done successfully and that makes sense. You know, somebody's gone before you and made a way.

That's what products are all about right, we've made a way. But apply yourself. I mean a product like *Elevate*, it's not about, 'Here's what we did, now you do the same thing.' It's about, 'Here's how we did what we did, now plug yourself in your market, your niche, plug your passions into it and use those tools'. But it's going to come out the other side looking totally different than what we've done.

**Tracey:** If you had to start over again, would you do anything differently?

**Joel:** Oh my goodness. Yeah, I would. If I could go back to 1995, I would buy a ton of domains that were one word domains. I would have sold the Classic Games for a lot more to Yahoo! At that point I was naïve and I just wanted to pay off my debt and all that. It was worth significantly more.

I would probably be a little less trusting with people. I always think the best of people and when you do that, there's those that don't have the same character that you do and they'll take advantage and they'll step on you every chance they get. Being used is never a fun thing. It's one of the pitfalls of being out there and having your name out there.

There's some days that I think, 'You know what? I'm just going to go underground and just do the other things that make me money and disappear from the public eye for a while.' At some point I probably will, but right now I still feel like, 'No, you're called to do this. You've got a gift, you need to exercise that gift, you need to, because this is the way I make a difference, right?

It's not about how much money I make. It's sort of like Donald Trump, who's had it all and lost it all. Your success is not a measure of how much you've got in the bank account. Success is measured by the impact that you had and when you get knocked down, do you stay down or do you get back up again?

**Tracey:** Is there anything that you do on a daily basis that you think keeps you on track to staying successful?

**Joel:** I brush my teeth twice a day! What do I do that keeps me successful? I tell my wife everything. She's my greatest confidante and my biggest fan and I make sure she knows exactly what's going on. I value her input and her insight.

I surround myself with people who are smarter than myself. I couldn't do this on my own. I have incredibly talented execs on staff here, operations people, systems engineers and programmers, graphic designers. You think I could do this or develop an application for an iPhone or even make a DVD set? I'm creative and I know what my goal is, what the outcome is, but I'm not skilled.

I'm skilled in very few things. I can speak, I can write, I can create and answer my email. I can play games. I can make a mess of things if left to my own devices.

I think when you have a team and you create an atmosphere that's fun—I mean, we've got monkeys in our trees, you know—when you create an atmosphere that encourages creativity and for people to exercise their gifts, it leads to so much productivity and so much excitement about the things that you're doing, that it's hard to fail.

**Tracey:** So do you have any top tips for people in a home-based business or those who want to get into one, whether it be on or offline?

**Joel:** Have an approach that is about bringing value. Always seek to bring value. If you come at it from 'How can I get people to pay me money?' then you're missing out on the key component.

There's a book I read twenty-five years ago called *Do What You Love, the Money Will Follow* and I believe that. Teachers are underpaid. People who are in non-profits don't get paid a lot. So I have to modify that a bit to say, *Do What You Love, the Reward Will Follow*, because it's not all about money. But in trying to do a business, if you're bringing value and you've got a product or service that people will buy— seek to bring value first. When you do that, people will respond by purchasing, if what you've got is truly of value.

**Tracey:** So where to now?

**Joel:** I've got a busy day ahead. I'm going to California to speak. I don't plan out too far ahead. In fact my calendar for next year is not even on the wall. I have nothing booked past December of this year because I fly by the seat of my pants a lot of times.

I kind of know the things we're working on, where we're going, but I have the flexibility to be able to make a quick turn to the left and not be committed to something for the long-term. Because you never know what's going to change. That works for me. That's not necessarily for everyone. Some people, they need to have everything scheduled out and if that's the way you operate because of your personality type, then go for it. It's just not the way I function.

## *After the interview . . .*

How are you adding value? Where is your passion? Something else Joel talks about is taking action. When you have an idea or knowledge, act on it. Go do it. So many people never do. Use your knowledge, share your passion, live your dreams.

You can tell a lot about people by two things. First, how they act under pressure. Second, the team they surround themselves with.

The day I interviewed Joel, it was a short work-week because of a public holiday in the USA. He had been working and speaking out of town the week before and was doing the same thing later that week. He was busy. He even tweeted that day that he was 'absolutely busy beyond busy.' Yet, he still sat with me. He didn't rush me and was totally present and focused during our interview. When we finished, he apologised that he couldn't spend more time helping me with my business. Then he had a thought, ran out of the room and came back with sets of his DVD packs that he knew I didn't yet have. I was just grateful for the interview and the opportunity to meet him in person.

The second way is through the people around them. You can tell a lot about a leader from their team. As I walked through the door, I was greeted by Joey, who heads up Joel's customer service centre and he showed me around. Another member of the team who really impressed me was Brian, Joel's executive assistant. Brian emailed me and talked with me on the phone prior to my arrival in the USA. He spoke to me the day before the interview to make sure I was okay, gave me directions and even recommended the best place to eat close to my hotel. I find that great people attract great people.

Joel is a living example of his trademark sign off 'Do good stuff,' not only in his business, but in his life. Thank you Joel.

For more information about Joel, check out:

www.JoelComm.com                    www.twitter.com/joelcomm
www.facebook.com/joelcomm      www.youtube.com/joelcomm

*Introducing...*

# Annette Sym

Annette Sym is well-known throughout Australia for her series of fantastic cookbooks '*Symply Too Good To Be True*' and for helping others to get healthy. She has sold over three million copies of her cookbooks in Australia and she is now making a name for herself in the USA with a new book written specifically for the US population.

Annette was my very first interview. So to say I was nervous is an understatement. Annette and her husband Bill live in a normal suburb, yet have an amazing home with an incredible view. By coincidence, they live just five minutes from my Mum.

When I arrived, Annette was on a radio interview over the phone. This fact didn't help my nerves, but the team made me feel at ease. Bill and I sat on the deck then Annette came to join us and we chatted for quite some time. This was the beginning of my journey to realising that these multi-millionaires are just normal people.

I chose Annette not only because of her incredible accomplishments, but because she is a Mum who took an idea and made it a success.

## *The interview with Annette Sym . . .*

**Tracey:** What I'd really love to start with is you telling us about your story, not just the story of how you created your business, but what led up to that.

**Annette:** Well it's interesting because when I look back on the past, I can see how I turned my greatest weakness, which was food, into my greatest strength. It goes back to when I was hitting the scales at two hundred and twenty pounds or one hundred kilograms and I was just really unhealthy and not really happy. My life was good, I had a beautiful husband and children, but inside, I just didn't particularly have a lot of pride within myself. It was interesting, when I got this photo taken of me walking out of the water in my swimsuit—that one little moment—was the turning point for me. Just one little moment.

That's often what it is when people look back. So when people ask, 'What was it that got you to be so successful?' I think, 'Well, if I hadn't had that photo taken, none of my story would exist from today.' It's really interesting how people often don't notice all those little moments as often they can be what really create big and exciting journeys for us.

So I saw this photo of myself in the swimsuit, cried, hated it, wasn't a happy gal and decided that the dieting was a problem. It was a reality check for me, because when I looked at that photo and saw this very overweight, unhappy woman, I saw a dieter and that's when I realised that it wasn't my fault at all, it wasn't my problem. It was the diets that were causing the problems, the stupid ways I was trying to lose weight.

I turned it around and said, 'Okay, if I gave up dieting, how different would my life be?' and it was like, 'Wow!' I felt this whole weight lift off my shoulders. But then what do you do? Because you kind of have to have something else as a plan. You can't just say, 'Well, I don't diet.' Then do I just get fatter and fatter and someday weigh three hundred pounds? I decided *no*.

I just know what I really want is to be healthy. So, that's what I thought—that's what I needed to do. It's give up dieting, become a healthy person. I did exactly that. It's just a simple thing really. I could talk for hours about what a healthy person is, but for me, at that time, that was when I changed my whole thought process, my habits, my pattern that I was in.

I have never dieted since. I lost over seventy pounds, which is about thirty-five kilograms in twenty months and I've been in my healthy weight range now for over seventeen years. That's the key, you know, it's not just about losing the weight, it's actually saying goodbye to it forever. That's what I teach people. Little did I know that all of that was going to help me become a gazillionaire, or that's the future plan. It was just to me. It was a personal journey and I took that personal journey.

**Tracey:** So what led from that to creating your cookbooks?

**Annette:** I was working for Weight Watchers as a lecturer. I did about four meetings a week for them. But at the end of the day, I was working for the love of helping others and I decided that I wanted to be working for myself. I think a lot of people can understand that. I wanted to work from home. I had young children and I decided I wanted those dollars in my bank, not theirs.

So I thought, 'What could I do?' I was thinking about doing cooking classes because at that time, going back many years ago, people thought low-fat was grilled fish and salad or if it was anything else, it tasted like cardboard. I was very confident that I could turn the whole scenario around.

So I put together this class. I went into a school and said, 'Can I hire out your home economics block?' Then, I thought 'Well, you know, I'm not going to make a lot of money from doing this.'

It wasn't really about making millions at that point. It was more just to make my time worthwhile. I was sick of working from pay to pay. My husband had a good job, but we just were never having any extra cash. I remember our freezer died on us and I thought, 'Well, now what do we do?' How do people have money in the bank where they say 'Oh my freezer's broken, let's just go buy one.' We certainly didn't have that experience at that time and so I was hungry for just being able to survive really easily.

I thought put the cooking classes together and then I thought, 'I know, I'll put a little cookbook together'. In those days, it was like pull out your computer and peel the edges off the sides, staple it, sell it for five bucks—this is how it all started. It's so humble, when I think back. I started putting my recipes together—that I had hundreds of—and it was like, I suddenly went, 'Maybe this is good, maybe this is really good.'

The cooking classes completely got forgotten and this cookbook took me over. It was just like an obsession from that moment on and has been to this day. That's how book one was created, just by looking at an opportunity that I was trying to create and putting add-ons to it and there you go.

**Tracey:** What did it actually cost you to get started?

**Annette:** Having had all those grand ideas, 'Oh yes, let's put a cookbook together'. No business acumen, no self-published skills, never put a book together. Anyone that read letters of mine knew that I wasn't that good at English. I just sort of knew how to do it.

It's funny when you're on your purpose. When you're doing what you're meant to do it seems to just be very natural how it comes about.

Often when I say to business people, 'When you're flogging a dead horse, maybe there's a reason for it, because it's not worth going through with.' Maybe you're at the wrong time or on the wrong path, maybe you've got to look at it a bit closer and not just keep thinking, 'Well, I'm determined I'm going to do this'.

Yes, determination is really important, but you can be crazy with it. I found that's what happened. I just knew exactly what to do. I really think the key to it was that I was my own customer. Any time, whenever I do anything, I go, 'Well, the old Annette, what would she have done with it? How would she have reacted to it?' I mean, because that's still me.

So when I started writing, I thought 'Okay, we've got to do this, we've got to do that'. Of course, we had no facilities at home, so it's amazing how you can provide when you have no income. I used this old kitchen bench that we had remodeled and made into a breakfast bar and we'd kept it. So I put that onto a really old desk. This was the office I'm talking about, off the family room, this little tiny area. I thought, 'Well, okay, there's not enough bench space'. So I got my ironing board and it was brilliant because it would go up and down with me. Sometimes I'd be standing and I could lift it up. The other bonus— you're going to love this—it was covered with a lot of paper, so I couldn't iron. 'Oh, no, I can't mess it all up, I'll have to iron another day'.

We really had a humble beginning. It really was. I had no money, so I did everything myself. It's amazing how when you're really determined, passionate and excited about something, how you just drive yourself to three o'clock in the morning to complete a job.

I remember I had to hire a computer to put the recipes and information on a disc, that was a floppy disc in those days. I remember paying one hundred dollars a week for that computer and it nearly killed me.

I had never typed. I'm a fast typist now, but I was the speed of Godzilla on that thing. I'd be up until three in the morning because I wasn't going to pay for another week. I said, 'I'm cashing this in on Friday, they're not getting another hundred bucks out of me.' I didn't have a computer or anything to start with, so it's amazing how you can make it work for you if you're determined.

Then doing a print run for the cookbook. How did that happen? I went to the bank and they just looked at me as if I was Dracula. You've got no actual income, you're self-employed with no one paying you anything, you're unknown, so here you are wanting to be an author but no one knows you, you're not Margaret Fulton. You have three children and get out of here. It was just ridiculous. I did the next best thing and I borrowed the money from in-laws.

In another way, it could have been just as scary, but they were fabulous. They had just come into a bit of inheritance and they were happy to lend it to us. I paid them back in six months. So that was really good. That's the thing. Opportunity just came from where you would least expect it. Bill's parents have not been wealthy people by any means and yet at that time, they had that little bit of cash flow that they could share with us. So, it was meant to be.

**Tracey:** That's it. It's amazing isn't it. I like to think of them as fine threads—the things that could or couldn't have happened. How many people would have walked into a bank and heard 'no' and they would've given up on their idea.

**Annette:** That's right and the funny thing is, I was speaking at a Home-Based Business Summit in Canberra with all the politicians and all the heads of the banks. They had two guest speakers, but they were home-based business people and I was one of them.

I remember I shared my story and I didn't hold back on the bank. I didn't particularly say which bank, but just saying that tells you which one it was. At the end of it, when there was a question time, one of the heads of Home-Based Business came up and said, 'Well, how would you react to Annette now if she came in?'

A home-based business in those days was people putting things in envelopes, or it was a hobby. But now a home-based business—well, we're big time—and it's probably the thing that people want most of all is to be a home-based business, because it's got so many benefits to it.

It was interesting to hear the responses, 'Well actually we probably would have wanted a good business plan from Annette and if she had been able to show that, we hope to think that we would give her that chance.' Because had it not been for my in-laws, we would now have no story. If I hadn't borrowed the money from them, where else would I have gotten it from? So maybe the journey would be the typical written book in the drawer. The dream dead.

**Tracey:** What do you think is the greatest skill that you have acquired over this time? What's the skill you didn't have that you really developed?

**Annette:** I think definitely business skills. The business skills came to me. My father was a very entrepreneurial business man in his own right. I am very much like him. I am just very passionate about what I do. I think having that work ethic where you just really commit to something, and I think seeing it through. For me, probably the biggest thing was not just resting on my laurels and saying, 'Okay, well there's the book.'

Basically, that's when the work starts—the marketing. It's learning how to market yourself, your book and your product, but then also reinventing it.

I've written five books. I've got quite a few other products. It's about continually growing and advancing, and not just being stagnant. I think that's probably where I'm that 'entrepreneur', if you want to use that word, and my biggest asset is, continually growing.

I think that we are at the cusp now of some greatness. With the launch into the US and all the other opportunities that are coming to us, I see only great strength and advancement. I don't see me slowing down at any point. My kids have said, 'Mum, you're getting old, are you ever going to slow up?' and I say, 'Maybe.'

**Tracey:** I was going to ask you about the US, because in Australia you have written three million books and I would say that you are at a celebrity status in Australia. So what prompted you to actually think about launching into the US and taking on that challenge?

**Annette:** I don't know whether I could say that I was getting a little bit bored, it's probably not that. It's just that I was looking for more. I thought, 'Well I've really achieved a lot here in Australia'. What I've got is, I feel, so valuable to people. I feel my product, if you want to call it that, is really important. It's really life-changing for people and with the illnesses that we have right now, with the health issues, diabetes, the obesity, cholesterol problems, and heart disease is the biggest killer in both America and Australia—I can help. So I'd feel a bit selfish if I didn't share it with America.

**Tracey:** Bill and I were discussing that outside—about that epidemic—and even the fact that I had read somewhere on your website, that when the economy is having a bad turn, people's weight increases.

**Annette:** Absolutely. Well, the reasons behind that are that people then eat poor-quality food because their budget for recipes and cooking and also for supermarket shopping, becomes much smaller.

They will buy poorer quality meats, so they're fatty. They often eat a lot of bread, pasta and potatoes to bulk up their meals. They're getting a lot of carbohydrates. Maybe fruit doesn't get chosen, especially the expensive fruits you would go for more in the season, but still, it might be just apples and oranges—so people don't bother to eat much fruit then. And stress. I mean when you're in economic times that are really tough, you eat, often out of stress. Who doesn't? I mean emotional eating is a very big issue with people who are overweight.

My heart just says, 'I've got to do more'. And, I'm prepared to do it. I'm really excited to go out there and work hard so that I can help people. I really feel so strongly about what I do and what can happen to people, because I see it every day. We get emails and people write to us, or I meet people on the street and they tell me they don't take medication anymore because they're so healthy. Their life changes. When you lose fifty pounds, it can really change things in life.

**Tracey:** Has there ever been a time when you just didn't believe in yourself or what you were doing, when it sort of seemed hard? If there was a time, what did you do when you got to that point?

**Annette:** Not really. Not really, because I'm very much about intention. You know, what is your intention and if you think, 'Oh this is really hard', then it is. I always sort of say 'Fake it till you make it.' I love to look at the positive side of things. I just naturally do that and so the only time I thought was really hard was in the beginning when I was distributing through newsagents and they took a while to really acknowledge that this was a product that they wanted to carry.

Up north in Townsville, I'd get phone calls. I'd be doing radio up there and they'd say, 'I'm trying to find your books, but no newsagents have them.' It was just awareness, but now of course, they all have them. It didn't take too long.

Maybe that first year was a little bit hard just making sure that there was supply for the demand. It's very frustrating when no one's got it in that town and you're doing a radio interview or you're on the Today Show, or something like that, and no-one can get them. It really is great when you have that support from the retailers as well. And I do now, I have great support.

**Tracey:** And do you find with the internet, that's also helped? That people can go online?

**Annette:** Yeah, well people don't hesitate now to buy online and we've got a great little business with the website. It's fabulous. It just keeps going all the time. I like to encourage people to buy out of the shops though, because I want those retailers to benefit as well and then if they're getting lots of sales in, they'll be more inclined to keep stocking.

**Tracey:** Going back to probably more at the start, you said you had three young kids, you were married, working off an ironing board—it must have been crazy? What did you do to balance that whole work, life, house, mother? Were there some strategies you used?

**Annette:** I always looked at more quality than quantity with the kids. Some parents are around 24/7 and they never really talk to their kids. I tried to make a point of weekends. Weekends are really important to keep to yourself. When you're a home-based business, sometimes that can be a bit of a challenge.

I really, really tried to avoid that, especially on a Sunday. You should not be checking emails on a Sunday. I think it's about just valuing what you're doing and valuing your family more in a sense.

What I did as well is that I did talk to my girls about it. We have three daughters. I remember sitting around the table saying to them that there would be times when I wouldn't be around because I did a lot of touring interstate when it went national and I said to them, 'There are going to be times when I'm not going to be around for you, but then if this really takes off, then we're going to have all these advantages that we just don't have now.' I went through all the advantages of having Mum being successful. I also said to them that this is something I really wanted to do and I explained to them why I wanted to do it. Then I got them to sign a contract.

**Tracey:** You got them to sign a contract?

**Annette:** I got them to sign a contract. I only ever had to use it twice. When one of them was whining about something, I said, 'You signed the contract.'

Sometimes when the kids have got an assignment and Mum's not there to help, they don't care about anything but what they need Mum there for. I think just having that contract sort of made them know there was a reason behind it.

Then, every time when something happened, we had a fantastic holiday somewhere or we went on a shopping spree to buy new clothes for the season, I'd say, 'Let's say thank you to the cookbook. The cookbook got you this.' I constantly reminded them that this wasn't just normal, that this all came from the fact that I had the job of writing cookbooks.

**Tracey:**  If someone was going to get started in a home-based business, what do you think are the vital ingredients for a person to have, to actually turn that into making the millions?

**Annette:**  You definitely have to have a bit of discipline, because when you work from home you can suddenly have the TV on in the background and there's a great show on and suddenly you're sitting down and three hours later you go, 'Ooh, I'd better get back to work.' You've got to have that discipline of being able to monitor your time. Not putting a lot of the domestic stuff in while you're working, like, 'Oh, I'll go and put the washing out.'

Friends are a nightmare sometimes. God love them, but they just pop in and don't think.  They say 'Let's have a chat' and you might be on a deadline or something like that. It's really hard to mix that up together.

I think having that discipline and treating it like work. Yes, it's fantastic in summer to be working in your swimsuit and your sarong and that type of stuff. There's some incredible bonuses of being a home-based business, like it takes me one minute to come to work. I can look as daggy as I want to be some days and as fabulous as I want to be other days and it's up to me.

Whereas when you've got to go out to work, you've got petrol, you've got the car, you've got all those clothes that you need every day. So it's such a great thing to be a home-based business, but it's not always suitable for everyone.  And if you have young children at home, that can also be a challenge.

There are a couple of things you really need to do if you are thinking about being a home-based business. One is you need to have a separate telephone line for your business. You do not want an important deal coming through and little Johnny picking it up and saying, 'Oh, Mummy's doing a pooh.' You don't want that. You want to have a separate line and you tell your children, 'Under no circumstances are you ever to pick that phone up.'

I also say to people sometimes, if you've got two of you in the business it's good.  If it's a husband and wife or you've got two friends doing it, or two business partners, and if there are young children that each day someone is delegated the children.

Say, for example, if the phone does ring, if the kids are making a noise or whatever in the background, someone is in charge of keeping them quiet while the phone call is going on. That means you're more professional. You can't have kids screaming out, 'Mum, where's my poppa?' A little bit of that's okay, but not if it's taking your concentration away from important phone calls. Especially when they're little ones, two and three-year-olds, they don't understand any of the wait for Mummy, they just want 'now'.

Having a door to where you run your business is really important. If you've got a home-based business and you're just going to have it in your lounge room, it's going to be real hard. You want to be as professional as you can as well, but it's the clutter. It's the spreading stuff all over through the house. It's just not organised enough. It means that when things are like that, you actually think a bit cluttered as well.

Having a room designated for your business and not spreading it through the whole house. If it's on the dining room table, that's going to be hard for the rest of the family when it's dinner time.

I understand for some people, you can't do it any other way. If you must, have a box where everything gets put into it, so you've got it neat and tidy when the next day you come to bring it all out. I just did it off the family room at first. Then we built the home here, where we've got, I reckon, the best home-based business in the world.

We're growing out of it now. We are getting too big. We have the three of us in there now and we could probably do with a fourth, but there's just absolutely no room and so we're going to have to work on that one.

Saying that, look at all the by-laws and the council rules for having a home-based business. Each council is different, you can only have a couple of people working for you if you do a home-based business, because if you've got lots of cars out in the road, your neighbours could complain; you could get in trouble with the council. You don't want to do that.

**Tracey:** What would you say is the biggest success you feel you've accomplished?

**Annette:** Oh having given birth three times is probably at the top of the list. Ouch! Business-wise, I think winning the Telstra Australia 'Micro Business of the Year' was pretty powerful.

That memory is always very strong in my mind for 2004. I won other national awards, but that one, for some reason, really did it for me because it's such a highly recognised one in Australia and the other finalists were exceptional. I was really excited about being there.

I won the Queensland award and then I won at the national awards in Adelaide. I remember meeting the other finalists and I went, 'Damn, they're good' and I just thought, 'Oh whatever, you know, whoever deserves it will get it'.

When our name was called, it was just a magical moment. For me, being the fat kid (I was an overweight kid as well), I never won any trophies when I was a kid. I was really good at physical culture, but all the little skinny girls got it. I was saying to people, 'This is my time to shine.' This is for me to show that I'm not just a good cook, there's much more to Annette Sym than just being a good cook. Yeah. I'm getting goose bumps.

**Tracey:** So could you describe what a typical work day is for you?

**Annette:** I'm down by nine, sometimes I'm up at two and four and one in the morning when I'm doing radio interviews in America, but just generally I'm in the office by nine o'clock. Rhona comes in just after me. Sometimes I'm in earlier if I've got a lot going on, on radio, it depends, but generally about nine.

Bill is in the office very early, so he gets everything started up. I'll just check my emails, see what I've got on the schedule at the moment, like, for example, we're adapting a twenty-eight day mind-body weight loss program I did for the Australian website and I'm working on that for America now. I'm just changing all the terminology and the recipes and the program, just for America, and that will be launched next month.

I'm off to the United States. It's just phone calls, radio, keeping up with all the things that we have. We do a newsletter every month and we're just doing one actually that's supposed to go out today for the US, but it's the first one. I don't know, as you do in business, just keep doing all the things you do and the day goes. Normally I finish work when someone yells out, 'Dinner's ready.'

**Tracey:**  Does it feel like work though?

**Annette:**  No, that's the thing. You see, that's why they've got to yell out for me to come out for dinner, because I could just sit there all day and night, it's terrible.

Normally, by then I've had enough and I'm quite happy to sit down and watch mindless television for a few hours and just relax. I mean there's so many great things that we do. I do a lot of interviews with people and different media things come along. There's always something going on, it's incredible.

Like, if you ask my office manager, it's not work. We just have so much fun with what we do here and it's just really exciting. I do a lot of speaking as well. I'm a keynote speaker, so I'm speaking next Tuesday afternoon at the Innovation Centre down at the University, on business. Then on the Saturday I'm doing this Expo, so there's planning to get ready for that. I do workshops and lots of other speaking.

**Tracey:**  Bill was saying that you're speaking to two lots of a thousand women in the States over a weekend.

**Annette:**  In Kansas, yes. I'm excited about that because I just love to talk. I feel like I've got a message that I want to share and I like to do it with humour as well. So we have fun. I like to have fun there.

To me, it's about the people sitting there in the audience. How can I get them to think smarter? How can I get those people to challenge themselves to say, 'Well, yeah, maybe I'm not doing it right and I can do it better.'  For them to actually say, 'I deserve to be really healthy. Why am I resting on feeling just okay?'  If you want to lose weight, 'Now is the day that it all happens.'

**Tracey:** Obviously, that's why you're still doing what you're doing. A lot of people would probably say, you know, you've done it, you've made millions, you live in the beautiful house with a happy family, but you're still doing what you're doing; obviously, there's going to be that passion and that love in there.

**Annette:** Absolutely, I love it, love what I do. I feel very honoured to be on the journey that I'm on. I don't do any of it for the money, I really don't. I know that sounds , 'Yeah, right. Whatever.' I mean, I certainly love the benefits of working hard and being successful. I'm not going to disagree on that one at all.

When I do things, I always think about the value of it to somebody and I know that if it's value that I'll be rewarded. I just love helping people. I'm a Taurus. I'm the earth mother. My husband just keeps telling me my credit card's not going to bounce, so that's all I need to know about. I have no idea, if someone said, 'What are you worth?' I have no idea, just ask Bill. I believe that's the big thing. When I see someone in business just for greed, I don't think they make good choices, they don't make good decisions and they never last very long.

**Tracey:** So how do you know? Think back to the early days when you just got that real spark. Was it just, I don't know how to even articulate it, but was it an inside feeling? Was it just enjoyment, happiness that came across to you when you built it?

**Annette:** I think it was that I had a clear intention. I could see the path. I knew where I had to go and what I had to do. Every time I've done something, I've always known. Like when I went to go to America, I just knew that I needed to do it. It's a knowing and just having that confidence.

I always say to people, when you fear something, you doubt it, you give it the wrong sort of energy and the wrong sort of strength. Whereas I always think that I'm going to succeed and it works. I'll just sort of go, 'Okay, well let's do this, I reckon it'll go really well.' If I hesitate, as I always say to people, 'Go on your gut feeling.' If you ever need to know an answer, just go within and just say, 'Okay, how am I feeling about this?' and if you're going, 'I'm not really sure', then don't do it.

It's when you get that buzzy little feeling and the heart beats faster, or you just get, 'This is really cool'. That's when you know you're onto something. When I look back over the decisions I've made, I think that's what helped me, because I have listened to my gut feeling.

I can remember, for example, when I was looking for a distributor. I know that's probably one of the most significant things that helped me succeed. If you asked me that question, I would say getting the right distribution company. You can be a self-published author, but it's 'How do you get it out there?'

You would never want to be self-distributing. You'd never want to do it. It would be a nightmare. Yes, you can still publish, but to distribute you really need powers behind you.

I remember going to one company and they knocked me back and said, 'You're not Murdoch. We're not interested. You know, who are you for God's sake? You're a woman on the Sunshine Coast. We don't know who you are, go away.' I can remember thinking, 'Oh, bugger', for about ten minutes. Then I went, 'Well, obviously, you're not the right ones'. They weren't the ones that were meant for me.

Then I approached someone else who happened to be owned by Kerry Packer, which I kind of thought was pretty secure. That family worked for me. I remember going to them, meeting the manager and she 'got me'. She said, 'I get you Annette. I see that you're not just going to put this book out and say, 'Well there you go, it's a lovely book.' I had a plan of how I was going to attack the media and do all these things and she really helped get me onto that.

I remember the phone call. She rang and said, 'The head guy, the manager of Network Services (which is the company that is distributing), is going to ring you on Monday with a decision. He's got the book. I've rung him. He's going to look at it over the weekend. He's going to ring you on Monday.'

Now that was the longest weekend of my life. They distribute to all newsagents and I knew that they would be the turning point. I knew that if I got them, it was going to be, 'Get ready, here we go!' The other alternative after them was Random newsagents with a much smaller distribution chain who had already said they would love to have me, but they were much dearer as well. It wasn't ideal, but I did have that as a backup if I needed it.

I can remember when the phone rang on the Monday morning. I remember looking at it and just thinking, 'Oh God, this is going to make or break me.' You want to answer it, and you don't. I picked it up and he said, 'Hey, Annette, it's Mark from Network Services'. My whole heart, everything, just shut. I just said, 'What do you think of the book?' and he said, and I remember it as if it was yesterday because it was the most important phone call I'd ever had as far as my business went, 'You know what? I think your book is spectacular. We would be honoured to distribute your book.'

I'm one of those people that cry at everything, but I was so excited I couldn't cry. It was just so fabulous. I thought, 'Oh my God, I'm just so excited, I can't cry'. It was just too beautiful. I knew then, that moment, I said, 'Here we go, here we go, Annette's in.' Here I am today with nearly three million books sold and I'm one of their top ten publishers.

**Tracey:** If you had to start again, is there anything you'd do differently?

**Annette:** Probably buy a separate ironing board!

Probably I would have maybe got my husband into the business quicker than I did. He was a head chef, so a lot of people were saying, 'Oh my God, he must have helped you cook' and I go, 'No, because when you're a chef, you do a fourteen-hour day. You don't do cooking when you're at home.' So I've always been the cook at home, but I needed to get someone else to help me.

I did too much on my own for too long. I probably wished a year earlier that I'd got him in. It really did help once I got that extra support. So probably that would be the only thing.

It was okay, it still worked out. It was a big decision to say, 'Okay, you're now going to lose that income.' You know what I mean? That was a big decision to say, 'Okay, you're going to come work for me and I'm going to pay pitifully, but I'll give you so much sexual harassment you'll love it!' I think he thought he was semi-retiring. Ask him how hard he works.

**Tracey:** I really believe that people who have become successful have some daily disciplines they do to really help keep them at that peek of success and believing in themselves and knowing that they're heading forward. You talked a bit about intention, are there any sort of daily habits or things that you do to keep you on track?

**Annette:** Well, definitely eating healthy. What I preach, I do. If anything, I'm even more disciplined with myself than I would expect, say, for you. I really do live a very healthy lifestyle, drink a lot of water.

Probably the discipline I have is making sure my inbox doesn't get too crazy. I get a lot of emails and I get really overwhelmed when there's a lot just sitting there waiting for my response. My office manager and Bill will answer a lot of them, but there are some that Annette has to answer and if they're sitting there and there's a lot of them, it worries me a bit. So I try and keep on top of that.

I remember one time we were really busy and everything was going on and I just said to everybody, 'Can we just stop for a minute?' because we were all getting quite bothered and tense with it. I said, 'Aren't we popular. Look how everybody wants a piece of us and how well the business is doing.'

They all just looked and went, 'Yeah'. I said, 'We're really busy because everyone loves us, isn't this great?' And instead of just going, 'Oh, this is getting crazy', it just shifted the whole thing.

So I try to really look at everything as a wonderful experience if I can. There are days when I get tired and I just say, 'I'm sorry, I'm going up to my bed for an hour' and I'll come back a new woman. Especially when I'm writing columns for newspaper and trying to really focus on a lot of intense work. I always say, 'Don't try and flog yourself if you're tired, go and have a break and come back.'

**Tracey:** If someone came to you and said, 'Oh, I just couldn't do what you've done', how would you respond to that?

**Annette:** Well, you can't if that's what you say. I would really love that person to say, 'I don't have to be *you* in it, but I can be me and fabulous. I can really do whatever I want.' Just like we've done.

It's about how you think about yourself and really having a good plan. You've got to do your research. You've got have the confidence in your product and believe in it. If you're trying to flog something you don't believe in, then forget it.

But also, I was talking to someone this morning about it, when you're looking at your own business, you've got to understand that you might think it's fabulous, your family might support you and say this is the best thing you've ever done, but would a stranger spend twenty bucks on it, or whatever price it is? That's what you've got to do.

Your family, love them to death, but they're not the people that are going to make your business successful. It's the word of mouth of people who have no idea who you are. That's the one thing that I love is that people tell others, 'You've got to go and get these books, the *Simply Too Good to be True* lady, she's got these great recipes'. That's how I've succeeded. The people have driven my success and I just have such gratitude for that, that people love to tell other people. That's the best compliment you can get, I reckon.

**Tracey:** There's a lot of talk in the media and people just talking on the street about the economy and I see that that's sort of an area where a lot of people are now looking to the home-based business. What would you say to those people about listening to those things about the economy and how that will affect their business?

**Annette:** Well, once again it's about—what's your product about? How smart are you with your spending? I think that's where you've got to look a little bit more closely at what you spend your money on.

I was talking to someone the other day that's trying to launch a new business and she has spent money on a website that was awful. That's all I can say. She spent money on someone promoting something for them like a PR company to send out press releases that did a dreadful job.

She said, 'I just feel so wounded right now that I've spent all this money and I've got nothing from it and now I've got to go out and do it all again.' I said, 'When you met the web people, did you believe in your heart that they were going to do a really good job?' And she said. 'Actually, I was unsure. I really wasn't sure, I was a bit worried.' And I said, 'Well, see, you didn't listen.'

When you're in your own business, every dollar you spend you want to justify that it's gone to something worthwhile. A lot of people when they work with corporates are used to having the logo'd pens and all the little bells and whistles that go with corporates because they can afford it. When you're self-employed, you don't do any of that. You know what I mean? You just spend the minimum that you can and try and do as much yourself.

Outsource though where you need to and I absolutely believe in that. I think that you cannot be the front of everything. I know that I have lackings in certain areas and that's where I employ someone that's amazing at it, to do it for me. So making sure, that if you do involve other people and you are spending money, make sure it's going to be money well-spent.

**Tracey:** Is there any other advice you'd like to give to people if they were going to start in their home-based business, or if they've already got one. Is there any other pearl of wisdom you have?

**Annette:** I think, use the media. The media is just so great to really help you go to that next level should you need it. I say to people, when I started, that's what got me going. It was just getting all that attention through the media and then people going to the shops and saying, 'Oh, I saw this lady on TV, she's got this cookbook which has got guilt-free chocolate cake. Where is it? Give it to me.'

That's what you need. Awareness. People need to know about you. Doesn't have to be national, it can be your free local paper. You can ring them up and say, 'Oh, look, I don't know whether you'd like to do a story about what I'm doing here in my home-based business.' They love that.

Local papers, the free papers, for example, if you're doing something significant or something important, let the media know about it, because they have to have stuff in their papers, don't they?

The other thing is that when you look at your business, I'd ask you 'Well if you're looking for free media, what have you got to tell the media that they haven't heard before? What is it that they're going to go, 'Oh, wow, tell me about that!'

It's not about saying, 'I've got the best cookbook that you're ever going to read.' They're going to go. 'Oh yeah, whatever.' Every author has written 'the best book'. Everyone that's created a product—it's the best product in the whole world. They hear that all the time. But what's so unique about it? What is your point of difference? That's what the media want to know.

That's how you work out your press releases and things like that. What you write about that grabs them to ring you and to do an interview. Because free media is just such a great way to spread the word about your business and especially when you're in a home-based business and you've got no money.

Advertising, I don't believe in a lot of advertising, I don't think you get the value back. If you have a particular product or you're selling yourself in a sense, do what I did in the very beginning.

I used to go out to all the clubs. For example, whether it be the Lions Club or Probus or, as I did, the weight loss, non-profit clubs. I went out three times a week and I would go and cook a recipe and they all got to sample it. I'd say to them, 'I'll come and do it for you if you let me sell my books.' That's how I started. I call it my apprenticeship. It really was my apprenticeship and then I got the media coverage and the word just spread, spread, spread, spread, spread.

I'd go on tour and I would go out the front of newsagencies in the depths of a Geelong winter and I'd be out there with my little wok. If you knew the things that we've done to promote. We certainly haven't just sat up in the clouds, just putting dollars in the bank, I'm telling you. We've worked hard. Really hard to get it. But I've enjoyed every second of it.

So if you want free media, you've got to think of something really unique about yourself. Mine was my 'statue', the swimsuit, the fabulous Annette in the swimsuit at two hundred and twenty pounds (one hundred kilograms).

When I rang the media and told them I've got this life size statue of me in a swimsuit and I'm this wide and that tall and it's a really good example of what I used to be like. They'd go, 'Really? Wow' and 'That's sexy.' That's what they call sexy in the media. I know she's anything but, but it's the actual topic. When something's sexy in the media it's like, 'Oh, tell me more.' They're interested, you've intrigued them. You don't just give them facts and you don't just ring them thinking. 'Well, I'll get some free publicity'.

Go in as if you're going to give them a great story. The media are about stories, about what will the readers want to hear or read. What will be the television shows people want to tune in on Channel 7 at five o'clock because of that segment. It's not like, 'Let's do this so Tracey can have a free ad.' It's nothing like that.

You know, that through it all, somewhere along, it might only be one line, you know, her cookbook is *Simply Too Good to be True* or the website, you get the website in. It's all you need to create a buzz about your business to follow up. So think about what is unique, what is your point of difference.

**Tracey:** Where to now for Annette and *Simply Too Good to be True*?

**Annette:**  Well, you know the world's waiting for me, I've got a lot of travelling to do. Obviously I want to conquer the US. I'm just waiting for the call from Oprah or Ellen. They'll have me at 'Hello.' Yep, I'm ready for them. I've worked out my outfit and everything.

This is what it's about. Look at the future. I'm very goal-orientated. Like if you have a look in my office you'll see my latest goal poster and it's got the things listed and I'm about two thirds of the way down, crossed-out and I'm thinking by the end of the year I'm going to have to write a new one. That's kind of exciting and I do one for about two or three years. About two or three things on it and I think that's really important.

As a home-based business, you need to be driving yourself and looking forward to your future and conquering these baby steps or whatever you call them to get to where you want to be in the end.  So looking at where your goal is really important.  I always say to people, 'If you don't know where you're going, how are you going to get there.' So your goals poster—I call it my goal poster—I get them to write it up. Can I tell you a quick story about that?

**Tracey:**  Absolutely.

**Annette:**  I was doing this show, a business morning breakfast show on Sunday, *Your Business Success*. I was the, what did they call me?—The legend—I can never remember—the legend. I was a legend and I was helping another small home-based business operator.

So they flew me to Melbourne and I met this girl and her husband.  They were just in the early stages of their business and up to now they're just really surviving and we were talking about goal setting.

We were writing a goal poster first. So we got the cardboard out and she did the heading goals and I said, 'So now, just on a piece of paper, I want you to write down what are your goals, before you write on the cardboard.'

She's going through the different things, and she said, 'I want to go on *A Current Affair*'. I said, 'Oh, that's fantastic, you should get on *A Current Affair*, this would be perfect for them.' So she said, 'I'll write that on the poster.'

I said, 'Just wait a minute, you're going to write that down, that you want to go on *Current Affair* and that's a fantastic goal to have, but sometimes,' I always say to people, 'you've got to be careful what you wish for, because you may not wish hard enough.' What about the *Today* show? What about *Sunrise, Kerri-Anne, 60 Minutes*, don't you want any of those? And she went, 'Oh yeah.' 'But you're only writing *A Current Affair* down. What after that?'

She said, 'Oh.' It's like that concept of thinking, that broad thinking. I said, 'How about instead of writing *A Current Affair*, you write down, 'I want mainstream media.' So she wrote that down. She phoned and she said, 'I had *A Current Affair*, but also I've got …' She was listing them off. Blitzed it really well. She wrote it down.

She had two small children, so she said, 'I want an Alice.' That was from *The Brady Bunch*, you know, Alice. She said, 'I want an Alice.' So she knew what that meant. Other people would go, 'You want an Alice? What's an Alice?' Alice Springs, like what? No, no, no, I want someone to come in and look after the kids and us, so that we can be the entrepreneur business people. So she wrote me a list of all the things that they wanted and it really worked for them.

That's what I do, I always look to what is it that I have to do. In my personal life I do it and I do it in my business life. My health and well-being, am I going to make sure that I walk so many times a week and make sure I drink lots of water. I have a list of all those personal goals that I do on a daily basis, but then I also have the business, which is a very exciting one.

So it's about America, I want my own TV show here and in America. There are things in the pipeline leading me to that as we speak. I can't say too much about it. Obviously, I'll create more cookbooks in America, I've only done one. I'd like to do another four, so they've got the five.

I see the TV show as the big catalyst to really take me to that next level and that's what I'm working towards. I'm also now an executive producer of an Australian film. Cookbook author, now executive producer of *Mind Fire* it's called, it's a thriller. It's an international film that's being completely filmed here on the Sunshine Coast.

**Tracey:** That's amazing. How did that come about?

**Annette:** Well, that came about because I've worked with a few different cameramen over different times and this particular cameraman he told me once when he was doing something for me, that he'd written a movie and I said, 'That sounds really good.' He said, 'I need backers and all this sort of stuff.' I said, 'Oh Gareth, good on you, mate', that sort of stuff.

He decided that maybe I should be one of them. He and Andrew, one of the other guys, pitched to us about it. I read the script and I went, 'You know, what? This is fun.' I'm just thinking red carpet right now. The bling, red carpet … all the film premieres!

I just thought it was a great thing, because we're very financially successful, to not only do something that's a great tax deduction, but to actually do something that's completely out of your realm. Also, actually because of our commitment to them, it really got the whole thing happening and I loved that.

I'm a hope-giver, you know, with weight loss and that. I give people hope and I was giving. I wanted to do that in anything I can. So these people, having that funding helped them. I don't say it was the catalyst by any means, but it certainly helped them be able to go on and do it. I like that. Why not help other people create their dreams. If we make gazillions out of it, I'm okay with that too.

## *After the interview . . .*

Intention and action. These two powerful words, when combined, can create a powerful business. Annette is a master of both.

After the interview, Annette took me into her office and showed me her goal poster. If you have chance, view the goals of someone who is at the top of their field but still growing and moving forward—it will change how you set goals forever. Her goals were huge! Yet she had already crossed off most of them, which left me no doubt that she will achieve the rest in record time.

She also had quotes on her walls. The one we discussed at length was:

> *Don't look to become a person of success,*
> *Look instead to become a person of value.*
>                                                    *Albert Einstein*

Annette is right. She is a hope-giver. Wife and mother of three, she started on an ironing board and with passion and dedication she has continued her journey to great success. To me it proves that anyone can make it in a home-based business as long as they do the work and stay focused on what they wish to achieve.

Thank you Annette.

For more information about Annette, check out:

Australia:  www.symplytoogood.com.au
USA:  www.symplytoogood.com

*Introducing . . .*

# Stephen Key

Stephen Key is an incredibly talented man (not that he would say that) and also very down-to-earth. I first came across Stephen when he was a speaker at a seminar I attended where he spoke on licensing products and taking inventions to market—yours or someone else's.

Stephen did something that I have never seen before. Before the event started he was in the audience, mingling and talking to the crowd. He even spoke to me. When he was on stage, he seemed to just be having fun. He gave lots of fantastic ideas, stories and how-to's. Often speakers give minimal content and hope to sell you the rest. Stephen gave it all—so much that I couldn't write fast enough.

I approached Stephen to request an interview. I wanted to hear more of his wisdom firsthand and he didn't disappoint. I hope you enjoy his thoughts and learn as much as I did from this interview.

## *Interview with Stephen Key...*

**Tracey:** Can you tell us a little of your story and about how you got to be here?

**Stephen:** Well, by accident actually. I was in business, studying business at University and I hated every minute of it. I took a class, an art class, in college and found I loved working with my hands. At that point I knew I wanted to create. I knew I wasn't an artist, but I knew I wanted to make something. I wanted to be creative, but how do you make a living? That's the tough part.

My father gave me the freedom. He said, 'Stephen, whatever you do, find something you really love to do.' I'm surprised my father told me that, but when he woke up each day, it was Christmas for him. He loved going to work and I saw that and so it was easy for me to take that leap. But working with your hands, being creative, how do you make a living doing that?

So that's how I really got started, I took that leap of, 'I don't know exactly what it's going to be, but I'm going to try it, I'm going to try to do that.' I think that takes some courage. Well, you have to have a little courage to do that and some people have a hard time finding that. But if you can, you never know where it's going to lead.

That's how I got started and I just started making things and taking them out and trying to sell them. Of course, I wasn't very successful. Like anything else, it takes time, but I did figure it out. Eventually I tried it enough and I found out what people liked. I had to work pretty hard at it, because if you don't have something that someone wants, how do you make a living?

I learned a lot and actually, from that point on for ten years, I sold things up and down the state of California. Making things and selling them on a Saturday and Sunday. If it didn't sell I kicked it to the curb as fast as I could to find something that *would* sell. That was the greatest lesson I learned, that you really need to understand your audience and what they want. So, that was my start.

**Tracey:** So what were some of the craziest things that you have ever invented or made?

**Stephen:** You know, everybody says I'm an inventor and I don't think I am. All the products that I've ever come up with put a smile on someone's face. That's all I ever wanted to do, find something that was clever that would give a smile for a minute, so they weren't really inventions.

My first idea that made some really good money was called the 'Michael Jordan Wall Ball'. I love playing basketball and I did something that was so simple when you think about it, I just changed the shape of the backboard. I put Michael Jordan on the back, sent it to a company and they licensed the idea. That paid royalties for ten years, on an idea that was not protected. I did it. It was so simple, but it was different and it showed me that you don't have to reinvent the wheel. It put a smile on people's faces, it was one of those things. So, it's not really an invention.

But I have been lucky with some of my ideas that do solve problems and I collect royalties on some of those other ones too, but I'm not this big inventor. I just find opportunities and knock on doors. I even ask companies what they're looking for.

I think I'm fairly clever. I can look at something and I have a few skills that I learned along the way, that to be creative—anybody can be creative—you just have to look at something backwards, or turn it upside down, or ask what if it did this, or what if it did that?

Start thinking like a child. Sometimes we lose that ability, but if you do, you can look at something differently. It's just problem solving. Then I would send companies the product and if they liked it they would pay me.

**Tracey:** Why did you decide to stay at home whilst doing that?

**Stephen:** Well, number one, it wasn't a choice at first. When I was out of college, well, what do you do with art? I mean, I left without a degree and I didn't really have a skill, so I was going to create. I was going to create my job. I was going to make something.

That's how it started and I didn't believe that anyone would ever hire me, so I never even went for a job interview, until I was twenty-seven years old. I guess I've been always this way, making things at home, taking them out and selling them. It wasn't really planned, it was kind of natural.

Then I took that one job at Worlds of Wonder for a year and I didn't like it. I didn't like working for anybody else. I've been self-employed for my whole career. In my business, what I've learned is that you need to have some sales skills. I did a little door-to-door sales at college, just to pay the rent. When I was selling stuff up and down the state of California, that was sales too—I didn't know it at the time.

The number one skill I think you need in any business, especially for a home business, is you have to be able to talk to someone and have something they want. You have to reach out and you have to have some sales ability. If you don't have it, go get it! That's a functional skill you can learn.

Of course, some people are better at it than others. It's a skill that I think everyone should have because you have to sell yourself, no matter if you're getting a loan at the bank or if you're negotiating to buy a car, or whatever you're doing in life. Even if you're looking for a date, you're always selling yourself.

I wish people would realise that's the big part of any business, especially if you're a business that you're running out of your house. You're going to have to run it, you know, get up at eight. I work more than eight to five, because I love what I do, but I realise that I have to be very disciplined. But, when I have the freedom, I have the freedom to take time off when I want to. You do work like a regular job. I don't think it's any different. You might work a little bit more. I think you might worry a little bit more, but the freedom, like the gains, are so huge.

I didn't plan on staying at home, it just kind of worked that way. Now I believe where the future is going, my future anyway, is having people work for me, but they don't actually work in one location. They can work at their home, they can work wherever they want to work. I can have people work in different cities. I love the internet because now you can work with people all over the world and I sell online courses now that allow me to have a website. Orders come in and I have people that fulfil them and send them out. I don't even have to be there anymore.

I think that, for me, it is the business of the future. There's really no overhead per se. You need to have some tools, like a computer and you need to have some skills to set that up. But think about it, you don't have to drive to work, spend money on gas. It has a lot of positives, there's no doubt about it.

We do all our classes on GoToWebinar, so you're working with hundreds of people all over the country. Everybody's in a different location and that's what the internet has allowed us to do. So it's a good time in business.

**Tracey:** So you talked a little bit about what you're doing now. Could you tell us a little more about some of the things that you're doing in your business now?

**Stephen:** I have two different businesses. My primary business is licensing technology. I was very fortunate to see an opportunity. I read in the paper how there was never enough information on containers and I started to pursue this because I had an idea that could solve the problem. I'm not very good at solving problems, but it was right there in front of me, I couldn't believe it. No one else had seen this solution, it was like wait a minute, take this over here and put it over here. This is going to work and it did.

It took me some time. I had no idea about the industry and you don't really have to have all the answers—it's perfectly fine—just do it and you'll be okay. You'll peel back, you'll discover, but just do it. Take the fear out, throw it out the door. You're going to fall down, you're going to make mistakes. Who cares? Just get back on your feet again. Sure enough, that technology has been selling for about ten years.

What I really like about licensing is that it doesn't require me to be there. It doesn't require my hands and it has a multiplying effect. It has all those elements to generate wealth.

If you have a business where you actually have to use your own two hands, well there's only so many things you can do, right? I don't care if you're a doctor, I don't care if you're a lawyer. My father taught me, 'Whatever you do, if you like it, look at how many pay cheques you're going to get until you retire. Add it up, look at it and if you're satisfied with it, fantastic. If you're not, find something else.' Because there's no mystery in any of the numbers.

So I realised that I needed to find something that has a multiplying effect, because I really don't want to be there. I like to generate money of course. I like to have my freedom. The answer was licensing. Taking an idea and licensing it to a company who is basically renting the idea.

One of my businesses is licensing a product called Spinformation. It's a rotating label that companies put on their products. I piggy back, I sell the real estate back to them because it adds 75 percent more space What I really like about that particular business is that I can be standing here and every time they make a label I'm getting paid. If I can duplicate that to other products, because it has that ability, to go on multiple types of products, I can get paid from different sources.

But you have to realise, things go up and they come back down too, always. So you need to look at it, be practical about it. I like an opportunity that allows me to do what I want to when I want to. But licensing is what I'm doing today. That's my primary business.

My another business is educating inventors, entrepreneurs and business people on how to take your dreams and how to make them. How to find your passion and how to make a living from your passion. How to open doors and how to get companies to say 'yes' and how to get people to say 'I want to work with you.' All those things.

I have a partner. He runs that business for me and it does very, very well. We have a very good program where we do online classes. I speak about it and that's another one of those things I love to do. So I'm very content, I'm very happy that I found something that I can do that makes an income and allows me the freedom to do the other things I want to do in life. It doesn't require me to be there, or use these hands, so it's nice.

**Tracey:** What do you think has been the biggest skill you've had to develop over the years to be who you are now?

**Stephen:** Being confident. You know, I married a very smart woman. The smartest woman I ever met and she married me, so I guess I'm a pretty good sales guy. I realised there's some things that were lacking, skills I did not have, that she had. So maybe that's why I was so impressed.

We met at a company, she was basically running the company and I didn't know what I was even doing there. She's got a great education. The reason we moved out to a very small town was that she got a job at the largest winery in the world, vice president and this allowed us the lifestyle. I could start my business and we could start a new life together. I got married fairly late, she ran in a circle of people that I was very intimidated by. They were very smart, educated and here I was a guy just selling stuff. I felt like, how would I ever compete?

But there was a time we changed. I had a little success and I realised we all have our own strengths and we all are different and given a little bit of success, the day I became comfortable with myself, I didn't care what anybody else thought. I was comfortable with me and it allowed me to find my voice.

Once I found my voice everything changed. The fear of making mistakes or not saying the right thing just went right out the door. I deserve to be here just as much as anybody else. In fact, more so, because guys like that, eventually they're working for me. Guys that have ideas, they can look at things differently and are the ones that drive the things forward.

Someone said to me early on, it is the C students who have the A students working for them. I didn't really realise that until later, but once I found that confidence, it was really to say 'Look, I am just as capable. I have different skills than you have.'

We all have different skills, but I do believe if you lack a certain skill, figure out how you get better at it, or hire somebody, or find a partner that can compliment your skills. Because we all have little areas that we need to improve on. I have some big gaping holes, huge holes, but I also have some other people that fill those holes for me because I know what *I'm* good at. So just recognise your strengths and weaknesses.

**Tracey:** We were having a chat before we started about failure and I thought that was a great thing and I thought maybe you could share that?

**Stephen:** Failure. You know everyone has this fear of failure. When we realise that the stepping stones for success are failure, then you realise, 'I need to fail, I want to, a lot.' Once you get over that, you realise, 'In order for me to move forward in a project, I'm going to fail' and that's perfectly fine. Just get up and do it again.

Don't let it measure who you are, but realise failure can be your friend. It's not comfortable to fail, but it's when you realise 'I'm going to have to fail', that you start to look at it differently. Because it's like in sales. If I call on ten people, nine are going to say no, but that one person is going to say yes, so I want to get through the nine people as fast as I can. It's just the facts.

So it's a numbers game and it's okay to fail. I always look at this way if someone tells me no. I just think they just don't have enough information, or I'm not there at the right time, they're too busy, or finding that person that has that open mind.

Believe in what you're doing, have the confidence and have the enthusiasm that you believe in and find that right person that will say yes. If you don't, find somebody else, and keep looking until you find that person that says, yes. You can, it's just a numbers game.

Don't let fear stop you. It's so much easier for someone to let fear stop them. 'I don't want to call somebody' or 'I don't want to step out'. It takes no courage to say, 'I give up.' It takes a lot of courage to say, 'I'm going to keep on pushing ahead.' It still bothers me and I still get nervous when I make those calls, but I try to gather up. You know, people say, 'Steve, why do you still get nervous?' But I do, because I want people to like me, accept me. I want them to say yes. When I get a no, I hate it. But the only way for the no to feel better is to call someone else to try to get that yes.

You've really got to stay on top of it and don't get discouraged. No one's ever going to say anything. They're not going to laugh at you. They might say no. Go on to somebody else. So, fear, don't let fear be your friend, but don't be afraid of it. Use it, realise you have to fail. You know, failure is okay.

**Tracey:** Another little story I'd love you to share is about one of the things you do before you go and speak somewhere, which sort of comes from that fear, but actually turned into what I saw as one of your greatest assets when I heard you speak.

**Stephen:** I mentioned that I started doing a lot of speaking and before that I did zero. In fact, I had some really terrible experiences in front of large group and I said to myself, 'I will never speak in front of a group of larger than five ever again'. I was a volunteer basketball coach and my wife made me get up and say a few words to all the kids. I said, 'No, I don't want to do it.' She said, 'No, you have to do it.' I got up there and it was okay. I said, 'Okay, I could do this.'

Then I realised that I got so worked up, so nervous and I don't know if it was just excitement, but all these things, I thought 'How can I get rid of it? How can I ease myself down a little bit to get prepared?' So, I started to make an effort to talk to people before I'd have to go on.

If it was a speaking event I'd get there early and I'd start trying to meet as many people as I could. I'd shake their hands, look into their face and say, 'I'm glad you're here', say a few words and I got to know them. They got to know me real quick. When I got up to speak, I knew them. I could look at them because I'd already spoken to them. They were my friend. They were beginning a relationship, it wasn't like I was looking at someone for the first time and that allowed me to relax.

I do the same thing when I'm in a business meeting. I'll get there a little early. When everybody's kind of stand-off, I'll get there, I'll go around that room as fast as I can so they all get to know me very, very quickly, and it works. Even I've found myself at times in the media, in front of the TV cameras. I'm like a caged animal. I see myself pacing back and forth and so when I get on, before I go on, I talk to the cameraman and I ask them about what they're doing. I get relaxed. It just takes that energy out a little bit so then when the cameras roll I'm more relaxed. So find a way of just relaxing a little bit and getting that first word out of you, because if you're warmed up, it's much, much easier.

**Tracey:** I think the reason I wanted you to share that story was to say you could take a fear of something in your business and actually turn it into a fantastic asset by finding a solution.

**Stephen:** You know, I'm glad you mentioned that because I've had other people say the same thing and it does. It has turned that completely around to be an asset and people really connect with it and I do too. It works for me, works for them, so we're all benefiting from it and it's one of the tools that I just kind of figured out about myself.

Everybody always says, 'Steve, you look so relaxed.' The other trick that I've learned is to smile and that puts everybody at ease. I think that's the first thing we don't do enough of and I will try to do that when I'm shaking hands with people, I'll smile as much as I can and they warm up, I warm up. It's hard not to like someone if they're smiling at you. They're just little things that I picked up that work.

**Tracey:** Have you ever come to a point during your business career where you just weren't quite sure if you could do it, you had a bit of doubt?

**Stephen:** Every day! You know, I put a list together of what I want to do. I'm a visual guy—I want to see it. I want to see a list. I want to do this and this and this. I'll be driving in the car and I'm always thinking about what I want to go ahead. I always want to do something different.

In fact, I interviewed someone today that said the exact same thing that I feel, life would be really boring if I didn't do something new for me. I was one of those kids that couldn't sit still in school. I wanted to go, I wanted to do stuff. I think I put things in front of me that are challenges, that are almost out of my reach. I know they're out of my reach and I know they're going to tell me no—all right, I know that, okay—but I'm still going to try, because if I get a little bit further and then I can get leverage that to a little bit more, a little bit more. I find that I'm climbing the ladder of what I wanted to achieve. So I put together the list of all the things I want to do and I look at them all the time. Once I get one, I scratch it off.

Now those are long-term goals. I have daily goals that I get through as fast as I can because I like to feel I am very productive, I have to do that. But it's those larger goals that I'm really excited about, because you realise they take a little bit longer. You're not going to get them every day that you try. You try a little bit each day and you keep on trying.

I'll give you an example. Because I write for All Business—I'm trying to interview Suze Orman. She's very, very popular. She's a stretch. I get to interview a lot of interesting people, but she's kind of up there. It starts to get pretty high up there and I've kind of worked my way up and interviewed people and I really like doing that and she's told me no for a year now. Her people, not her, her people have. I got to her people, but not to her. So every once in a while I get a no. I'm always very polite 'That's okay, I'll check back with you later when maybe it's more convenient.' Then I look at their name there on my list and say 'I'm going to have to get her interview.'

Every time I'd interview somebody else, I'd always drop a little note, 'Hi, I just wanted to check back in. Hey, I just interviewed such and such.' It gets a little closer to her. So finally after eight months of dropping a note every two months or so, I get an email back that says, 'You know, I think we're ready for an interview.' 'You're kidding me?' He says, 'Call us back after Labour Day.' I thought to myself, that's one of those things that you just learn, that you just start with one piece at a time, and put it out there, but don't try to get it tomorrow or next week, don't put a deadline to it.

That's another thing I think people do. They put these expectations on things and they don't happen, they get discouraged. Just say, 'Look, I'm going to get that and I'm not going to stop until I do. I don't care how many no's I get because sooner or later I'll get a yes.' We realise all you have to do is that one time. Once you do that one time, you realise, 'I can do that over and over and over again.' You realise 'that's powerful' and you realise that's just a circle that gives you that confidence to go, 'I know the magic, I know how to make it work.'

I can apply those same principles to anything I want to do. I don't care what you want to achieve, you put it out there. You get the steps, you keep on working up, just keep going, keep going. Once you find that, there's nothing you can't do. I've told my wife there isn't a thing that I cannot set out to do. It might take a little bit of time. I'm very patient, it drives me nuts sometimes, but that's part of the process of the wanting to try to do new things that are exciting for me. If not, I think I would have to shoot myself!

**Tracey:** Have you had any major mentors through your business experience?

**Stephen:** I think that's actually a great, great question because I think we all need mentors or coaching and I think we're fooling ourselves if we don't. My father gave me another really great piece of advice. 'Whatever you want to do in life, find someone that's doing it, get as close as you can to them.'

I think people that are successful that have gone to a certain point in their career where things don't really mean anything to them, or they're trying to give back, and one of the ways they can give back is by helping somebody else.

I think you can find a mentor in any industry that you're in. Find that person and say, 'Look, can you help me?' Those are probably the most powerful words that you can ask someone, because that's really someone giving back. They're going to feel so good inside to help someone else—that is priceless. So whatever you want to do, find that person.

Now, if you're in the same town there might be some competition so find someone in another town. Make it so there's no competition. Find someone a little bit older that wants to give back. They will find that giving back is going to be very rewarding for them and they're going to want to see you succeed.

I believe a coaching mentor is the number one thing anybody should start out with and I don't care how old you are, there is always somebody else that can help you with some more advice.

So yes, I have one. His name is Steve Askin. In fact he called right before you got here. I've known him for over thirty years and when everybody thought I was completely out of my mind—he didn't. He is very proud of that I think. He looks at my career and says, 'You know, I remember when you started.' And I am proud that he's proud.

We have a very good relationship. His family doesn't even know him that well, which is interesting. I wrote an article about him and his family emailed me back and they said, 'Our father really gave you something.' They always thought that their father was a little different. I showed them a different side to someone that helped me. So I think mentors are important and I have mine.

You need someone to bounce things off of and say, 'What do you think about that?' A different perspective. Experience is priceless. If someone has more experience you say, 'Look, what do you think?' I know maybe some people think that shows a little weakness.

I'm the first one that says, 'Look, half this stuff, I have no idea what I'm doing.' The minute you realise that, you'll be fine. Realise you don't have to have all the information, but you know where to get it. Go after it and realise, 'I don't need to understand everything.' So a coaching mentor is number one on my list.

**Tracey:** So how does it feel, that the shoe is on the other foot? That you are also a mentor and a coach for other people?

**Stephen:** I'll never forget it. That's why I like the education so much. It's a labour of love. It started out as a labour of love. It's a business now, but if it's just a business, forget it. I take a lot of pride in coaching.

You know, we do online classes. I like to get to know my students, I like to know where they are, what's happening. I like it when they're successful and we have on our website what some of my students have done and I'm very, very proud. Now some of them have bought our course, but I have a lot of people I mentored that have not bought our course and I couldn't care less.

It's the journey that's really, really important. Someone was there for me and so I'll give that back, every time, no doubt. I think you'd find a lot of people would do the same thing.

**Tracey:** Have you ever had one of those moments that I would call a *Sliding Doors* moment? You know, where you could take one path or the other path and you realise, 'Hey, that was a real defining moment in time for me because I chose this path'?

**Stephen:** I guess looking back one of the biggest moments was when I was at a toy company. I found my future wife and we decided where we were going to live and I could have gone down to Los Angeles or Modesto, a small town. Modesto was a very safe place to raise a family, it was not very high profile.

I mean a lot of people ask me, 'Steve, where do you live? You live out in the middle of nowhere. Why did you do that?' Well it was safe for my children, it was safe for me to feel like I could play out in the big world but I could always come home. I know my neighbours and they know me and it's comfortable. So that was big. That was defining. That was one of those times, 'Do I do something that could be really fun but maybe not build my foundation that I wanted to build?' So I took a chance and I think it worked out beautifully.

There's been some other business decisions where you'd get to that fork in the road, 'What do you do?' and I've made some bad mistakes. I look back and sometimes you're so eager to say yes, you're so eager, that you know you should walk away and say no, but you just don't have the strength and power to say no. Saying no is very powerful, but you don't have the confidence to say no yet, because you think that opportunity will not come back again.

That has happened to me a few times and luckily I've gotten an opportunity to correct that. I won't make that mistake again. There was a big opportunity, it was with Coca-Cola on a project, which I wanted so much, but it wasn't the right time for it and it failed. I realised right then, sometimes you have to say, 'No, it's not right' and you'll get another opportunity. Now, when I have two different directions, I try to go both. I just say, 'Okay, I'll go this way and I'll go this way too. I'm going to go two different directions'.

So yeah, there are a lot of defining moments, I think we all have and you learn from experience, but trust your gut, always trust your gut, it's never wrong. If it doesn't feel right, it's usually not. Even though you might justify it's right, it's not.

**Tracey:** What was it like to be on *Dr Phil*?

**Stephen:** Nervous. That was real exciting because I remember when I got the call ... the *Dr Phil* show had called and they wanted me to be an expert guest. It was very, very exciting. I just jump into things and said, 'Of course, yes.' I didn't care what it was about, 'I'll figure it out later.' It was really, really exciting being given the opportunity, someone had called me and understood my career and that I had a voice and that it was important.

I know some of the other people they were looking at and they chose me, which really made me very happy. I went down there. They treat you great. They put you up in nice hotels with fancy cars and I brought someone that's very close to me that I work with, James. Any time we have a PR opportunity I always take him with me because they treat you a little bit like a star and I don't get treated like that all the time, so it's really fun. They do the hair, they do the makeup, they get you all ready, you're all nervous. It's all that great stuff and then you go home and it's like, 'Hey, it's all over.'

What was really a little disappointing was that it was so short. But it's always good experience, right? I met some really interesting people too. That nervous energy I talked about earlier? I remember I was in the waiting room with other people. I have a tendency, I just talk to everybody. They're probably thinking, *Can't this guy just shut up?* But I'm trying to get it out.

I get to meet all these people and it was very helpful because they were giving me some advice on PR opportunities and other things they do. So it was really kind of neat.

My mentor told me, 'Wherever you go, collect business cards.' He calls this, 'Calling of the Cards'. You never know who you're going to meet, I don't care where you are. So be polite and get to know them. So *Dr Phil* was very exciting, but I wish it was longer; maybe next time.

**Tracey:** You've actually had a lot of PR opportunities. You were also an expert on an inventors show in the United States?

**Stephen:** Yeah, there was a show called *American Inventor* and they called me up. They found me and they had me interview to be a judge on the show. I was very pleased.

I didn't get that part. I love the failure, you see. Sure enough later they called me and they said, 'Steve, we need your help.' Because they realised that I didn't have enough camera experience, I didn't understand what they were looking for, it was too early. But I did understand the process extremely well.

So they asked me to come back to work as a consultant to make sure everybody did what they're supposed to do, that the projects looked, well, that they did work, because they had a lot of money riding on the show and they didn't have someone behind the scenes to make sure everything was going to work.

I got to go down and work with some really great people and the producers behind the scenes and it was a great experience. They paid very, very well too. I was very surprised. That was one of the benefits, because I would have done it for nothing, but they brought me down there and I don't know, I just wanted to do it and it was fun.

I've done some other things recently. There was a big show here called *The Big Idea with Donny Deutsch*. It was very, very big. I was watching it in the evening and all these creative people, people bringing products to the market, would come on TV and I was 'I want to do that.' I remember saying to my wife 'I'm going to be on that show' and she kind of laughed at me and said, 'Yeah.'

I wrote about it on my *All Business* blog, which I write three times a week 'I want to get on the Donny Deutsch show and I want you to watch me.' I kind of put that challenge out to my audience and said, 'So the first thing that we're going to do is that I'm going to Google, 'How to get on TV'. Sure enough, I showed them an article, so I wrote my little letter and did everything else and sure enough, they called me two weeks later. It worked. They called me up and I went out to New York and it was a great experience, it was fun. Very nerve-wracking though, but it was great.

**Tracey:** Another one to add to the toolbox of things that you've done, of living your life.

**Stephen:** I've had so much fun. And everybody, like I said earlier, they said, 'God, Steve, you look so comfortable.' You just learn to ask the right questions.

Everything, it seems, has a process. How many questions they're going to ask, how long should your answers be. It's a format. Once you realise that format, you can get through it. I learned something in Australia. There was a publicist that got me on the *Today Show* and I asked her, 'Now I want you to help me. Critique me.' And she did. She said, 'You know Steve, it doesn't matter what they ask, you just deliver whatever message you want to say, that way you'll never make a mistake.'

She goes, 'Now they might look kind of puzzled that you didn't answer the question, but that's okay, they'll ask another one.' But it's really amazing and I've watched other people now, because if you have your message and you keep on giving your message, you're going to be very good at it. You're still going to be entertaining, it's still going to be good for TV and they're going to get what they want. But don't let them guide the interview. You guide what you want to say and that way you'll always be perfect. So that was really interesting advice.

**Tracey:**   So what's your message?

**Stephen:**   My message would be, whatever you want to do in life, just do it, have a fun time with it. If you want to be creative, go for it. Have fun and find that passion, find that drive, find that thing that makes your heart just pound.

Don't be afraid of failing. If you don't know exactly what you're doing, which is perfectly fine, find someone that does and get close to them and go for it. Don't let fear guide you. Just take fear and throw it out the door. So you'll make some mistakes, that's perfectly fine and you'll do great.

**Tracey:**   Is there anything that you do on a regular basis that you think helps you be the success that you are?

**Stephen:**   How do you measure success? I think that's an interesting word. For me success is freedom. I've learned that most people that are successful have had a lot of failure. Even though they might have been successful, it all comes crashing down too. So how do you do this right?

I think you don't try to get too high when it's high or too low when it's low. You realise it's all about finding that success, what is successful for you. That for me is doing what I want to do, having freedom, enjoying it and no matter what happens in the economy it doesn't matter to me.

I've set myself up very practically. I'm practical, because I've had enough lows to realise, 'Okay, things do go down.' So don't get too excited when you're up. Keep your head on, do the right things. Because it'll come back down again, so just be smart. At the very beginning of anybody's success (it happened to me), you go crazy. You overspend, you buy big things. Everything's got to be big. House is big, cars are big. You realise that does not last.

I think the older you get, you realise less is more. In fact, someone's been saying that there's going to be a whole shift, demographic shift. The older you get, you don't buy as many things, you don't buy new houses or cars, you get smaller. The last thing you do is want more work, you want less work.

I think that's what I've learned, just love what you do. So success for me is defined as really having the freedom to say, 'Look, I can walk away from any deal at any time.' I know that everybody is taken care of with my family and I'm never in a position of financial danger ever again. Those days are long over.

I think that comes with experience, that comes with having some failure. You realise 'Okay, let's just be smart.' I think everybody in the United States is learning this lesson now and it's a tough lesson for people to learn. Don't over-extend, be debt-free if you can. Everybody's got too many credit cards, so just be smart. Learn from your mistakes and work hard and enjoy what you do.

I don't think it's ever been about money. I think it's been about achieving those goals, those dreams that have been a little bit out of my reach. You know my Dad said, 'You'll be the richest man in the world if you love what you do.' So that was good advice.

**Tracey:** It's great advice. If someone came up to you in the street and said, 'You know what Stephen, I just couldn't do what you've done', what would you say to them?

**Stephen:** I would say that you can do anything. If they knew all the disabilities, if they knew all the holes that I have, I think they'd be surprised. Don't believe what you read or see on TV. Some of that stuff is all made up, so don't go by that. I think if you just work hard, you can achieve any dream you want to.

Now I know I'm not going to be President of the United States and I'm not going to be a brain surgeon. Okay, I know those things. I think we all can achieve some type of goals. Just find someone that's doing it and make a practical guide, get a roadmap. Someone said, 'Don't dream it.' I mean, you can dream it, but have a roadmap. 'This is how I want to get there' so you can see it. But just to say, 'I want to get there' and not have the roadmap?

It's amazing, I don't know why people do that. That to me says, 'You're going to fail.' And if you fail once, it's in your mind, you know what happens when you fail and you have this cycle of failure? That's all you think, that 'I'm not going to succeed, I'm going to fail.' You've got to break that habit and you've got to find out, 'Okay, what are the elements of success?'

It's finding that roadmap. Finding that mentor. Taking those steps and doing it very small and just being consistent. Once you get a little bit of success, then you realise 'That's how to be successful.' Then, before you know it, you understand.

I don't say there's a formula, but there's steps to it. I used to tell my kids, 'I know the magic.' They'd go, 'Well, what is it?' 'Well, I know the magic of success. It's hard work, being persistent, being dedicated, finding the passion, all those things.' But you have to have a roadmap and one that's realistic.

**Tracey:** You did mention a bit about the economy and what's happening at the minute in the economy. What would be your advice to people at this point in time who were either in a home-based business or looking to get into a home-based business, to push through this?

**Stephen:** Well, I think in every down economy, or up economy, I think there are opportunities. I think you just have to find what they are and just find someone that's doing it. Find someone that has that home-based business and ask them. Maybe not in the same town.

See, I think this is so easy to do. If you want to stay at home, if you've got kids that you want to watch over a little bit closely, you want to be at home, but you need some other income. Or you decide, 'Look, you know, I don't want to drive into the city, it's too far. I want to do something home-based.' Find someone else that's doing it. Either find them on the internet or ask about it at church or ask about it at your local town meeting. Ask them, 'How do you do that? What are you doing? How does it work for you?' Find that mentor that's doing exactly that.

That's how I would guide them because that's the best advice I think I could give anybody, just find someone that's doing it and repeat it. Can you imagine, by finding someone who's already doing it who's successful at it, they can give you all that advice you don't have to live through it yourself? This to me is the fastest way to success, getting close to someone that's already doing it.

So that's what I would say. I don't care what economy it's in. I don't care what town you're in. I don't care what city you're in. Find the other people that do it. Find what they're doing in another part of the country and say, 'All right, how are you doing it here?' Because there's a lot of people that are doing home-based businesses right now, I think it's on the upswing. People don't want to rely on companies, they don't feel secure with companies. Even if you are working at a company maybe find a time where you can start your own home-based business on the side.

I believe in having more than one business. Be careful putting all your eggs in one basket. Find a couple of different voices. That's what I really like about what I've done. In having a couple of different businesses. If one goes a little funny and one persists, it doesn't really matter. So I've protected myself and we're doing some things I've never done before too.

I've asked my team, 'Okay, go get the information. Find someone that's doing it.' See? That's it. We're working with some other people that I met that are doing something I want to do. I've just kind of got involved in it but I know I'm not going to be very good at it. We're making mistakes right and left. I know it and I don't care. Just don't make them twice. Ask.

I'm finding my mentor in another business right now. I think you can apply that to anything. This is how I like this message. I don't care if you just want to increase membership for your local organisation, how do you do it? Well find another organisation that has got great membership and ask them 'How did you do it?' Find someone else that's doing it and ask them exactly how to do it. Find a friend, find a mentor, find a coach.

**Tracey:** So where to from here for you?

**Stephen:** I'm going to keep on doing what I love to do. I know I have mentioned I have two kids in college. I have one who is going to be leaving very shortly for college, so I have a new life, a new career. Some people would be scared, but I think it's an adventure.

I think for me, 'All right, what am I going to do for the next twenty-five years?' Have a plan, get the plan and look at what other people are doing.

I like freedom. I like to be able to move about the country. I don't want to be tied down to one location. I'm going to set up some other people to really run my business. My business basically runs by a phone. I could go anywhere.

I took my family on a vacation for six months when they were a little bit younger and I just had a phone. I realised that's all I really need.

So for me, it's finding the right team of people that can execute what I want to do. That allows me to experience my next twenty years of just people, life, and places, and hopefully there's a book in me somewhere. I'm going to try that, that's going to be fun. I'll have my daughter write it since she needs the job and I don't write. [Stephen does now have that book – *One Simple Idea* available now from Amazon]

I want to do more speaking around the country and I'm not quite sure how to do it, but I do know I will find out. I will make mistakes, but I don't care because I will figure it out and we'll have fun with it and it will be another adventure.

**Tracey:** Will you come back to Australia and speak again?

**Stephen:** I will be back. I am doing a webinar, which is coming up, and they said they were going to bring me back in November, but I don't think it's going to happen because they've got some other people they need to work through. There are some other people that are pushing me around over this, some other speakers that have more experience, they're part of their team. They put me on their team but I'm like the new kid right. 'Come on, pick me, pick me, pick me.' But they're not going to yet, so I'm very patient.

I think I'm going to be back and I'm going to really enjoy it. In fact, I'm going to bring my whole family next time because there was so much to do and see and I loved it. The people were great, the experience was great. So I'll get that opportunity, but you've got to be patient a little bit and that's hard for me. I'm nervous, I just want to go. I thought they were going to invite me back in November, but I'll get there.

**Tracey:** It sounds like you've done a lot of really cool stuff. Is there anything that we've missed in these cool stories of things that you've done? You know, you've been on TV shows, you've gone to Australia to speak, you've taken your kids away for six months.

**Stephen:** It's interesting about that six months. You know how you get so busy and you don't really connect with your family? The kids are a year and a half apart. I said to my wife 'Why don't we just take off for a month and go someplace that has no TV.' She said 'yeah' and I was kind of surprised. I said, 'Well, why don't we just take off for six months?' She said 'Better, let's do it.' She kind of called my bluff. So I said 'Why don't we put the house up for sale and just go and see where we land?' And she said, 'I'm in.' Sure enough we packed the kids up, put the house up for sale, I had my phone and we just took off.

She figured out exactly where we were going to go and she had everything planned. We were on the road for 167 days. We went to seventeen national parks. It changed my life. I came back and I realised there really only is my family. I just didn't need the things I thought I needed. That was the life-changer for me.

At that time we had the big house and the cars and all the great stuff. I came back and got rid of all of it, every bit of it. I said 'I don't need it, I just want to be free. I want my family.' So that was a life-changer for me. The biggest thing, my wife is very smart and she knew it would be. I had no idea. First two weeks, I'm freaking out going, 'What did I do? Three kids in a car 24/7? I can't even get away. I'm going to go nuts.' In fact, I'm the only one that went nuts, everyone else was calm. It was like 'Dad, come on, we've got a long trip here, what are you doing flipping out?'

So we've done things like that. We've done other types of travel that I think was pretty exciting. I've got, I won't say the travel bug, but I love other cultures. That's my future, moving about, I really like that. We've got a trip to Scotland this year and we'll be in Spain. But we'll stay in a small town. I like getting into the small towns and not rushing and seeing things. Just to be. The flow of it is kind of fascinating to me.

I've been very lucky, being able to do exactly what I wanted to do and found someone that had the same goals in mind. My wife, I mentioned before, was vice president of Gallo winery. She quit that and became a school teacher, which is very unusual. She took a different change in career because she recognised that life's too short not to do what you want to do and she didn't like business. She said, 'I want to give back and I love education. I always wanted to teach.' Now she teaches sixth, seventh and eighth grades and has even started a charter school.

I live in a very normal neighbourhood and I've got a couple of firemen across the street and they're like, 'the weird inventor over there.' They don't know a lot about what I do, but every time they hear something they're always like 'He's a very unusual guy.'

So it's a very normal upbringing for my kids, but we've done some stuff that has made the world a smaller place for my kids. They understand and they've got the travel bug. But the same advice my dad gave me, I have given my kids, 'Look, I don't care what you do, just love it. Just love it and be. Give back, give back. You're here to give back.' I've got the best kids on the planet, so I guess that's my biggest achievement, there you go. That's my success, it's my family. Everything else is just kind of gravy.

## *After the interview . . .*

Have you had a moment in time when you have met someone or read something and you just know, right to your core, that you won't ever be the same? That is how I felt when I finally left Stephen's house that day.

Stephen was waiting outside for me when I arrived. We probably chatted for half an hour before and at least that long, if not longer, after the interview. He was not only generous with his time, but also his knowledge.

The main thing I got from Stephen was not to be afraid of failure. 'It takes no courage to give up.' I have that on my wall now. Such a simple statement, yet so powerful. As a home-based business owner, or anyone going after a goal for that matter, it is a great statement to remember.

I hope you can feel through Stephen's words that he just loves what he does. Energy just oozes from him and I find it contagious. People ask me all the time 'How do I know if I'm passionate about something?' The answer is simple, you will know and so will everyone around you. Stephen is a prime example of that.

A few days later, my brother watched Stephen's interview on video. It always amazes me how people get different lessons from the same information. My brother's lesson was not to put a deadline on your goals. Just keep going until it is done. What did you learn?

In our chat after the interview, Stephen recommended some books to me that I thought you'd like to know about too. They were, *The Magic of Thinking Big* (a personal favourite of mine as well), *The Purple Cow* and *The Tipping Point*.

To be in the presence of someone who loves what they do, has an abundant outlook and is happy to share all they have, is life-changing. Who could you find to do that with you? Don't be afraid to ask. When I contacted Stephen, I was a nobody. I hadn't done anything earth-shattering. I was an Australian writing a book and wanting to interview a few selected millionaires. Stephen's response was, 'Well, I started out as a nobody too and someone gave me a chance".

Thank you Stephen.

For more information about Stephen, check out:

www.stephenkey.com
www.inventright.com

*Introducing . . .*

# Craig Wolfe

Have you ever seen a product on a shelf and thought 'Who came up with that idea?'

When I first heard of Craig and his company, CelebriDucks, I was fascinated. Rubber ducks, like the ones you put in the bath, but in the shape or likeness of celebrities. Could there really be money in ducks? As you will discover. Yes, there is.

Craig's was an interview I was really looking forward to. Would there be a room of ducks? How do you get started in such a business? How do you not listen to the 'doubters'? Because I was sure most people would have said, 'You're doing what?'

This is an intriguing story of how one man found a passion and made it a success.

## *Interview with Craig Wolfe . . .*

**Tracey:**  How did you end up where you are today?

**Craig:**  I was one of those people growing up who really had no idea
what they wanted to do. Which was fascinating to my father who from
a little kid wanted to be a pilot. To think that you go through your
whole life and get to the point of graduating college and still not having
the slightest idea was amazing to him. He was intrigued, he wasn't
upset, he was more amazed. I've been the type of person that can only
move something when I feel passion for it. Otherwise, I'm just, you
know, doctor, lawyer. I think these careers are great for the people who
do them if they feel passionate about it. I didn't.

One day, I was in a store in Los Angeles and I saw on the wall a
picture of an original animation drawing of Mickey Mouse. These are
the drawings that they do before they make the actual animated cartoon.
The original artist's hand-done work. Then someone else colours it and
the then photograph it. It becomes Snow White. I looked at that raw
drawing and I was just captivated. I mean for some reason, I loved it. I
said, 'Can you actually buy one of these pieces of history?'

Make a long story short, I started a business almost immediately
buying and selling original animation art from these old 1930 Disney
cartoons. Source it out, find the best places to buy them, that was my
business. It started growing more and more and eventually I opened up
some animation art galleries in Europe. I kept doing animation related
things.

Then the 'California Raisins' came on the air, which were a big
phenomenon in the US. Those dancing raisins, everyone thought they
were made just for Australia, but they were huge here. It was really the
first big animated commercial ever and with Motown music behind it, it
was fantastic.

I contacted the studio and I ended up getting the rights to market
the artwork from the commercials. So I moved back from Europe,
where the studio was, opened up another museum gallery with all these
displays of clay animation and computer animation and things were
clicking along fine.

Then we wanted to market the artwork for the Simpsons. They were getting very popular. I thought our company could do a good job with it. We went down to Los Angeles, met with the network and here again there is a story with it. Other companies were in there, big talkers, with a lot of money and I wasn't willing. I've never been willing to just throw money and ridiculous figures out just to get a job. It wasn't going to happen with me. At the end of the day they went with the other company who is bankrupt today.

I made a detour into another niche, which happened totally by accident. I was walking down the street and there I pass a window at Macy's filled with all these old vintage Coke machines. The old ones from the 40s and 50s, the old coke bottles, before they were in cans, the old shape - all this memorabilia. I was dumbstruck. It was an epiphany. As much as you talk about a business epiphany, that was it for me. The whole feeling. What Coke represented and their advertising with refreshment in the old days and the good feelings you have. It was just so nostalgic and these machines were beautiful, they were works of art. I went into Macy's and to make a long story short, I bought the whole window display. They sold it all to me.

Then I called Coke. They were just coming out with the Coca-Cola bear commercials on television. I said 'I'd like to take your artwork and market it, the artwork from the commercials, just like Disney does with their animation from their cartoons.'

It was very big at this point. Disney animation sales were going through an extraordinary amount of money on the artwork, the original cells from Snow White or the early Mickey Mouse cartoons.

It took a year for them to finally grasp the concept and did they want to do it and this and that. Kind of like you were mentioning earlier, just say yes and figure out how to do it. These commercials were done on a computer. There was no way to get it from a computer onto acetate like a hand-drawn cell that I knew of, but I figured we'd figure it out. Eventually a year later they gave us the contract.

I started contacting all sorts of people and printers. I'm working with the studio who is doing the original animation, because we have to figure out how to get a high enough resolution. You know, the resolution you see on the TV screen can be much lower because there's light behind it. When you take a scene and put it in a frame, there's no light, so if you don't find a way to brighten it and then get it onto the acetate, it's not going to work. We worked with the original animators for the Coke commercials. I had my own orders and then printers and some of the top presses in the US trying to figure out how to get it onto acetate.

Make a long story short, right before the Coke catalogue was about to print, I got my first sample in and I looked at it and I framed it. It was framed and I hung it on the wall and I broke down in tears because it looked so dark. I failed. I had already printed the whole thousand of them and I go 'It didn't work.'

Then the Coke catalogue team was having a meeting, which was about fifteen minutes from here of all places. The catalogue team called and they said, 'Listen, something just dropped out. Can you get down here? Show us what you have?' I had this piece which was dark, so I went to the printer and at the last minute we figured it out, he figured it out. We pressed something behind it, so instead of having space where the light would be diffused, when it pressed up against it and up against the frame, it popped out the colours. Amazing.

I ran down there, five minutes to spare, walked in the room with it and because something else had dropped out, it went in the catalogue. *Boom.* Became one of the top-selling art pieces. Then we did it with the next Coke polar bear commercial cell. I must have done about ten of them, twelve of them. They're all just doing great. Funnily enough, the guy who ran the Coke catalogue, he now lives five doors down. Just bought a home, just five doors from here. I always tell the story 'Hey man, you kind of seeded my company."

When that worked, once I did it with Coke, it was easy. I go to Budweiser—the Bud frog commercials were just coming out, same thing, they weren't hand-animated. The Bud frogs were three-dimensionally shot like they were animatronics. We did with Budweiser what we did with Coke. So Pillsbury, Kelloggs, M&M, Mars. You see where it went. All of a sudden we were going.

We became the largest publisher in the country, probably in the world, of artwork from television commercials, all from that. I didn't have the slightest idea how to do it, but I figured I'd pick it up I guess, intuitively I felt it could be figured out. Not by me, an English and Religion major from Hobart College, but by other people and that's one of the key things any entrepreneur should know. Surround yourself with people a lot smarter and better than you. Don't try and be all things to all people because you're not. Know your liabilities. That's because I don't think that much of myself. The only thing I do feel I know is how little I know and now I know enough to get the help I need. I have a crew of people I work with who are just, you know, I'm in awe of their skills and I tell them—they're just brilliant.

It was going great and then one day a friend, probably a little inebriated, he had this idea. What about a rubber duck which is also a celebrity, a *Celebriduck*?

Normally you wouldn't do anything with an idea like that, but I had extra money, we were doing pretty well. The one thing about doing all the artwork for Coke and Budweiser, I didn't invent the Pillsbury doughboy or the Bud frogs or Coke bears, but in a lot of ways, your creative juices get stimulated. You kind of want your own brand, your own thing.

So I thought 'Hey, why don't we actually try and make one'. So I called King Features Syndicate, they own the rights to Betty Boop. You know how it is when you're on the phone with someone and they think they're talking to a crazy person. They're very polite, they had licensing for North America. Okay, you make your Betty Boop duck and get back to us. We'll never hear from you again.

But we did have the money and we had the time, so we actually found someone in Oregon who knew a factory in China who made one and then we sent it over to them. One morning, as I walked from one end of the house to the other, there on the message machine, there's a message saying, 'We got your Betty Boop duck. It's really cute. We'd like to talk.' That was the beginning of CelebriDucks.

We started playing around with it. We got the Three Stooges and we started expanding the brand. But what really took off, is one day I was sending out press releases, I was just sending them out occasionally to papers around the company. I sent one to the Atlantic City Press in Atlantic City, New Jersey and the reporter called me and said, 'Well you're in California.' He said, 'Why should we write a story about you?' I go, 'Well, I'm from New Jersey' which I am, not Atlantic City, but from New Jersey. So they write a little story about CelebriDucks.

That weekend, the vice president of the Philadelphia 76ers, who happened to live in New Jersey, happened to read about us in the paper. Always looking for unique and innovative promotions called and said 'Listen, I'm coming out to California, how about an Allen Iverson duck?' Allen Iverson is this great basketball player, who played for the Philadelphia 76ers. 'Can you make him, just like Allen?' Allen has an armful of tattoos you would not believe. They're extraordinary. They said, 'Can you match those tattoos?' and the cornrows, his hairstyles, his earring, the whole thing. I said, 'Yeah.' Once again, I figured maybe somebody could, at some point.

Sure enough, we figured out how to do it. I'm telling you, when we got done with that duck, that duck looked more like Allen Iverson than he did. I mean those tattoos matched exactly. If you saw the two of them walking together in a tub, you wouldn't know the difference. It looked great.

Huge hit, game sold-out. Chicago Cubs heard about it, they loved it. They had us do a promotion. They threw them out during the first pitch at Wrigley Field. Then the Yankees.

It just rolled, all of a sudden we had another company. Me, an English and Religion major from Hobart College, who still to this day cannot read a profit and loss statement. I told you I throw them in a drawer and I don't look at them. I sold off the animation part of the company and we became all ducks and never looked back.

We just kept growing and growing. We started doing custom work for different companies. Fortune 500 companies of their brand, mascots, then we did all these top collegiate teams in the United States of all these colleges and major universities and a professional sports franchise contacted us about doing their players. We just grew.

One thing I didn't grow into was a formal office outside the house, because I just love working out of my house. I've always loved it. Film crews when they come, they come to the house. In fact, one of the cameramen for VH1, when he came over here, because at that time I was selling, he actually wanted to see about possibly me buying his house and him buying mine. It was really funny. So we do real estate as we do these interviews.

I've always loved it. It's just a style for me. Working with people overseas, their day starts in your night. If I have to work at night, I'm here. I'm watching TV, then just go and have a few emails, go back, it's a style that really works for me. Since these days, I tell people, I can run my business at this point with a laptop and cell phone, I could run this thing out of a beach in Waikiki. I don't even have a cell phone, but if I had one I could. Honestly, it could be anywhere.

I thought I had one of those unique business models. I outsource 99 percent of what I do. 99 percent! Which is very unusual. So you have technically in this S Corporation, one person, which is very unusual. I thought I was kind of a lone wolf out here.

Then I was setting up a new business and I'll tell you how that started, another interesting story, but I'm setting up a new warehouse in Kentucky and I was calling references that the warehouse gave me.

Talking to this one lady about it and she said 'Oh yes, the warehouse is great. We love working with them.' I said, 'That's wonderful.' I go, 'Yeah, I'm looking at your website now, are you in Oregon?' She goes. 'Actually I'm in the Bahamas.' She works out of her house in the Bahamas.

I go, 'You're in the Bahamas?' She goes, 'Yeah. I realised we can live anywhere. So I decided, we love the Bahamas, so we just have to go there. I do everything and set up a company in the US, but I'm here in the Bahamas doing it all from home.' I worship her. She has taken the concept and I have never seen anyone outsource more, to a whole other level, the Bahamas! She's really doing this Waikiki story.

It's extraordinary what you can do out of your home. The thing is, when you're out of your home and in your own business, you can innovate, you can turn on a dime, you can move so quickly with new licenses or changes, companies come to us, they can get product on the market, we can take their work, we can move quicker than almost anybody in turning around a job. Also because it's our gig, we can start new things, like this thing with Hershey.

I had the idea, you know Hershey Kisses? I love Hershey. Milton Hershey has been one of my inspirations. I've read every book on the company. I don't read business books, I can't understand them, but stories I can read. Story of Milton Hershey, Ben & Jerry, Starbucks, how they began, Walt Disney, that's what I read.

I was a licensee for Hershey, I did artwork for them. Like with Coke and everyone else. So I went to the head of licensing not too long ago and I said, 'Listen, why don't we do a Hershey Kiss duck? Like a little duck, like he's popping out of the foil, he's partly in foil, coming out and the whole box is all like Hershey Kisses all over it and the duck's holding kisses.' She loved it. She talked to the person who buys for Hershey. Then they had stores in Times Square and Chicago and the buyer said, 'Yeah, that's great, I'll carry them.' Turns out, she goes, 'Funnily enough, I was in the bathroom cleaning up and I found this Ohio State CelebriDuck.' She's an Alumni of Ohio State University. She had one.

So it looks great, this is going to be great, we're going to sell to all the major outlets. Then she has to approve things through the actual brand manager for the Kisses, of the actual candies. Seemed like a slam dunk, everyone loves it. The last minute he said no. He didn't get the idea, the concept of the rubber duck, how it related. I said, 'That's so odd, there's something, there's got to be something here. I mean, it's so odd that this happened like this. What could it mean?'

We started our own brand. Everybody loves chocolate, so we're going to do a chocolate-themed rubber duck with our own brand, CocoCanard. Canard is French for *duck*. That's the duck you saw with the beret, the kiss on the cheek, the big candy bar. We're going to design the box like a French chocolate shop. Then we're going to do a box of chocolates. We found someone to do manufacturing for us and these duck chocolates are embossed with a duck and inscribed with CocoCanard. We found this gorgeous box and we did that like a French chocolate shop and then a whole other website. We even sent a Canardgram, a gift of chocolate, the chocolate duck, a box of chocolates and a personalised note to anyone anywhere in the country. Valentine's Day, birthdays, Mother's day, send a Canardgram. On the back of every CelebriDuck box, no matter, Elvis or Michael Jackson or anybody, it now has how to send a Canardgram.

All of a sudden, a whole new business was born, just like with the Coke artwork. Every time we hit a wall we just like, you know, when you've got your own gig, you just slide off into another direction and our company was suddenly reinvented.

We're coming out with the world's first ever totally recycled green duck and no one's ever done it. We have these slogans 'green is the new yellow' and 'reduce your carbon duck print' on the box and the box is all recycled. Sustainable rubber ducky. Then we set up this whole new website, Greengram.net, where you can send the green duck and we're launching a whole line of soap, all natural soap. We came up with our own brand, CanardVert, French for *green duck*. Beautiful soap, best I've had. A recycled note on recycled paper. You can send a Greengram to anyone in the country. There's now Greengrams, Canardgrams. It's a whole new thing.

That's the beauty of when you have your own gig or a home-based business. It's not getting a board of directors. You're sitting around with friends, 'Yeah, they're going to work, let's do it'. Intuitively. I've never made soap, I've never made chocolate but intuitively, just like with the artwork for Coke.

I'm not what you call a fearless person. I consider myself moderately fearful actually, but when it comes to certain things, I feel no trepidation. I cannot tell you why. I can already see, like when I saw those Coke machines. I could see the end product. I had no fear that I'd not figure it out. I'd do it, it would be great. Sometimes when you find your niche and 'you've found your passion', you're fearless. You're maybe afraid about a lot of other things, from funnel-web spiders, to mice, to whatever phobic things, but when you find your passion, usually you're invigorated and you just find all this energy and capacity that you never knew existed. Then you find things come to you, the people, the answers, you suddenly psychophysically link up with the answers in what you need, because you're so open emotionally. You're not closed in, fretting and worring or thinking what your boss is going to think.

**Tracey:** It's just the most amazing story and I know people ask 'Well, is there any money in ducks?'

**Craig:** 'Does he make a living at this?' Actually the funniest story is I got a phone call once from one of my guys, who I advertise with in their magazines, he goes, 'If you're the largest publisher of advertising artwork in the country, or the world, how come whenever I call on the phone I get you?' I tell that story to everybody. I tell them, that is the greatest comment. I genuinely enjoy talking to people, I actually like to answer the phone.

Companies with voicemails and a million other layers or a company where you can't get to a live person, that's the company I'm not buying from. I like people. I want to connect to a person. So maybe that makes us look a little old-fashioned, but I don't care. I love it. It works for me. Celebrities who call, I pick up the phone. They're even surprised I answer. I'm surprised they're calling.

**Tracey:** What sort of process do you go through to find the best outsourcers to match what you're doing?

**Craig:**  Get references. That's number one.  That's your best bet.  Two, look at the work they've already done. What type of stuff they've already produced and get samples of the work and see. Three, spend time with them. Even if it's on the phone, do they feel like somebody you can work with? You get a good feel from someone and then you can ease into it and then do a little business and it grows more and more.

I made my mistakes, especially overseas, that's the toughest place to outsource. It's a whole other country. Another language, another mindset, so that's taken a long time to weed my way to the best people, the best factories, sorting communication issues, really getting a crack team.

You're going to have some bumps in the road, everybody does, but what are those scars. That's wisdom, hard-fought wisdom that you learn from. I would think that most home-based businesses do a significant amount of outsourcing and if you're afraid of that, good luck! What are you going to do, like have a hundred people in your home?

One nice thing, your home business is kind of your home. I mean some people have the space for offices and people, which is cool, you know? For mine, I just don't happen to need that. In the early days, when my daughter was home, she would be working here designing, that was totally different. But to think of a whole staff, all the people working for me, all here, it would be a little bit much.

**Tracey:**  So you were saying earlier about the process of actually getting a duck on the shelf. It's not like a 'Hey, let's do this duck.'

**Craig:**  Had I known, I never would have done it.  I'm not just saying it as a cute comment, I honestly wouldn't have done it. I know how difficult it was. I knew how hard it was to get that artwork from those computers, onto the acetate. How hard can it be to make a rubber duck, right? In America, every house has a rubber duck so how hard could it be?  Very hard. Very, very hard.

First of all, our ducks have larger heads, they're caricatures, so there are floating issues. Then to get it to be soft. In the early days we had squeakers in there to get them to squeak. And the packaging. I can't tell you how many renditions. I showed you four different renditions earlier, but they didn't hold up in shipping.

Then you make a production run overseas, I got prototypes in. This duck is floating on its side. 'Don't worry about it.' That's the big thing I was told, don't worry about it, it'll be fine when it arrives. You know what? It wasn't.

I can't tell you how many ducks that I was not happy with. Too hard, didn't float right. Because the CelebriDuck, to me, you should be able to throw it in on its head and it pops upright. Ninety percent of our ducks are like that. In all honesty the factory said, 'I really think you're pushing it here.' I'd really shrink the head of the ducks and my artist pushed for keeping his way and I should have realised the factory was really right on that.

I made mistakes, but by and large, it was really a hard learning curve to get to where we are today. It was a lot of learning curves. As I say, it wasn't just 'Here's the picture, make the duck'. Well, if there's a licence, you have to get an approval. This process can go on for weeks, months sometimes, back and forth, back and forth, change this, change that. Then you do sculpting. Then you have to make a wax mould, then you have to make a production mould, then you make an actual pre-production mould, then a production mould, and a spray mask mould for the painting. Then you have to do the box artwork, logos, trademark issues on the duck.

Let me tell you something—it makes the artwork stuff that I thought was so hard, like a piece of cake. If one duck ever makes it here, it is always a miracle to me, when I know what it actually takes to get through production.

Those first Elvis ducks in the white jumpsuit, with the little sequins. We were trying to get to Graceland for the anniversary in August. They celebrate his passing every year and it was an anniversary of sorts. I don't know if it was a twenty-fifth, I can't remember what it was. We were trying to get it for that date and it was so tight.

It's those little things, there wasn't a spray mask you can make that would allow you to do that little circle on the Elvis costume. There are 108 of them. So 108 of them, on five thousand ducks, had to be hand painted on. Hand painted 108 of them. You think anyone is going to do that in the United States?

I made my stuff overseas because all types of moulding, everything, painting, it's all gone overseas. You can't make my product here anymore. I have to outsource. China, whatever else you want to say, does some of the finest work in the world. So if you can find the right people, you're going to produce a phenomenal product.

Our factories are audited, we're part of the fair labour association as far as our employees are treated. We really are a member of all these things and do all that. It's a great group of people.

It took us a long time to figure it all out. So, yes, ducks were very hard to figure out, but we did and I'm glad. Now, in hindsight, I'm really glad I didn't know what I was getting into because it's the most fun business. It's how a business should be. You should wake up every day and go 'Far out, you know, this is cool, what's going to happen?' Yeah, it's fun. How many people can say that?

**Tracey:** Has there ever been a time when you doubted yourself or what you were doing and wondered if you could push through and make it?

**Craig:** Well, the Coke one I told you about when our first Coke piece came in, I felt like a total failure. I really did cry, honestly. I was so screwed up. But out of the ashes we resurrected ourselves.

When I got the first ducks in, it was disheartening. They were bigger than I wanted. There's a certain size to me that works. Too big, they're clunky. Too small, they're chintzy.

We weren't hitting it on the first ones. And the packaging. They couldn't figure out how to make the ducks stay in the box, right? You wouldn't think of these things. They glued it in. They glued it in to the point where it wouldn't come out.

I had them in front of me and the packaging was clunky and then the ducks, even though they were glued, they would still bounce against the plastic and there'd be a transfer of paint onto the plastic. These are the first ones I ever did. They were too hard. Paint's ending up on the plastic window that you see and they're glued in so you can hardly get them out. When you do get them out, the cardboards comes off with it. Welcome to my new business.

We stayed with it. We got better and better and better and it's one of those things where if you love what you're doing and you like the concept, you'll figure out a way to persevere to work out the kinks.

Let me tell you something. I've also studied a lot. Remember I told you I read, I read stories of business? It astounds me. One of the greatest things I've learned from all my studies is how many failures these products were that you look at today that are successful, that were downright failures in the beginning.

My main artist, Chris Howes, is brilliant. His father was one of the inventors of Silly Putty. Silly Putty was a toxic toy in the beginning. He was the one who came in and made it so it can use materials that make it a safe toy and keep the same material, the viscosity and the things you like about Silly Putty. He had to completely rework the whole thing. So he's really one of the inventors of it. If you go back to Silly Putty, you go back to so many foods, soft drinks, you would be amazed at how many were failures in the beginning. Not just food, but musicians. I've studied it all. How many groups in the beginning were just going nowhere? Even the Beatles. It was just a fluke thing that one of the things got picked up or something happened or one person had faith in them.

So all these famous musicians and products, they all went through a learning curve. It's very rare that someone just ran out of the gate. It doesn't happen that way in real life. Maybe in a story book, but not in real life.

You don't read about that, you don't hear about that. When you look about, you see the brand and you go, 'Oh it's always been like that.' No, it wasn't. They had to go through a lot of R&D, back and forth, lots of mistakes, releasing products and recalling them back in.

By reading, I got a perspective. I realised that I wasn't alone, that it's kind of a learning curve and it's okay. For me, every time I have something fail I'd go, 'Oh God, our reputation's ruined forever.' But you know, it's really not. I mean people eventually get it together, when you become maybe massively well-known. Hopefully by then you've gotten most of your bugs worked out. I think we have now.

**Tracey:**  What do you think is the best skill you've developed over the years that's helped you the most?

**Craig:**  Well this is going to sound funny, I mean being a Buddhist of sorts, a practicing Buddhist, can't speak much about practice, but I'll say one thing I've learned from my teachers and it's probably helped me more than anything else. It sounds funny to say it as a business, but *compassion.*

In my early days I was a hell-raiser. If things didn't go right, I'd be kicking ass. But over the years, I've found there's a better way to work with people and start to feel them, feel what they're going through and it's not taking things so seriously.  Everything changed. As I stopped taking things so seriously and stopped getting up on people for mistakes, psychophysically things would open up, things would change, answers would come, the right people would drop into my life and all different things would happen.

I've always done interviews. I've mentioned a lot of business interviews. What I've always tried to stress is *so goes your mind, goes your reality in front of you.*

Not getting into a lot of psycho-babble, it's just kind of a physical reality which probably in the most simplest way you would notice that when you're happy you probably do notice that things around you do tend to work out a little better and when you're really depressed and angry you tend to run into a lot of situations that kind of enforce that. It's not like any magical philosophy or new ageism. It is a psychophysical world. Things are interconnected.

So compassion and seeing that things are interconnected, does give you that space to kind of flow with things a bit and that's a really great position to be in. Because corporations, by definition oftentimes, are very motivated toward one thing, profits. They fire people and they downsize and if you don't do it you could lose your job.

People are always afraid of losing their jobs. But in a real business that's run more compassionately and really has a different point of view, there's more humour, there's a different feeling in the work environment, it's happier and things work out. You may make a million dollars, you may not, but you'll be happy and the people you work with will be happy to work with you. I always tell people, as an entrepreneur, don't lose that. It may seem trite, but to me it's the best business thing I could ever tell anybody, as far as the right disposition to enter into doing a business. It's not to take the world by storm, to take your brand and be the king of the world.

A lot of people have done that and they're not happy. They may sell more than you, but they're not happy. That doesn't mean that it doesn't count. To be successful as an entrepreneur, yes, your business is successful, but also your life is successful, you're happy doing it. People are happy working with you. That's the big picture and to integrate that into your business makes your life and your business one entity and that to me is one key point.

**Tracey:** If someone came up to you on the street and said, 'I could never do what you've done', what would you say to them?

**Craig:** Well, you're looking at somebody, as I said, English and Religion major, Hobart College, no idea what he was going to do, can't read a profit and loss statement, no business background whatsoever. Obviously if I can run a business, anybody can run a business. So, anybody can do anything actually.

True, I can't do brain surgery and you could probably sit and teach me for the next hundred years and I still couldn't pick it up, but everybody within their innate capabilities can find something they feel passionate about and make it work. They can. Everybody has the capacity to find something they love. We're wired that way to find what we love and if you love it, any human being can find a way to make it work.

I don't have to be the artist, I can't draw. Walt Disney wasn't such a great artist. He produced some of the greatest animation the world's ever seen because he knew what he wanted and so he knew who to work with. That's one thing an entrepreneurial business person can do. If you know what you want, you can find people who can help bring your vision to life, because you can guide them into what you're looking for. Anybody can do it. You can do it. So, yeah, I never feel like anybody can't do anything.

**Tracey:** You've touched on it a few times, on a couple of books, what would be some of your favourite books that you've learned from and what did you learn from them?

**Craig:** Of course, anything to do with Hershey, because I love chocolate. I recommend you eat it every day. The story of what Milton Hershey did—that man, you know how many failures he had? I mean, if you saw him, it makes my failures look like successes and he kept going. He found one person that believed in him.

When his bank note was due and it looked like his business was about to go under, there was one man who believed in him, who stood by him and gave him the money to do his initial production run, even though he had an early string of failures behind him, but he felt something about the guy, 'Maybe there's something here.'

He had sent a big order to London and the day the note was due—he took a chance sending it overseas—his money came in. The rest is history. He paid off the note, paid off the investors. That guy became a lifelong friend, his closest confidante and friend and Hershey chocolate took its place in history forever after that.

I read books like the Hershey story and of course the way Milton uses money. Do you know he started an orphanage? Milton Hershey is famous.

That chocolate company supports an extraordinary orphanage for underprivileged children. Maybe it's the largest in the country. It's endowed by that company. So, it's phenomenal, his altruism, the way he set up the business. Very inspirational for me. It actually inspired me, that in the future of my business it is all going to non-profits. It's like Hershey did. I think it's a wonderful model, I'm inspired by it.

Then there's the Ben & Jerry story. They tried to create a business that was not your typical corporate business. Their central thing was to do good in the world and to always give back. Phenomenal story. I've read all the Ben & Jerry books.

I know Starbucks has become a major brand now and people tend to not like the corporate things about it perhaps. But you read Schultz's book, *One Cup at a Time*, and it's fascinating, the birth of that whole company.

The history of Coke, any major brand, I've read the books. All the great brands, I love them. I learn so much from them. Maybe what I learn most is how they took failure and turned it into success and they hung in there through the belief in a product. What it was to incarnate a product. Because it's hard to birth a new art form or a new product. There's a million products out there, there's a million of them. Everybody's screaming for consumers' attention. So for you to feel that you have value in your product and to be able to stay with it, take the time to read the stories of those who went before you who were able to persevere—it's very inspiring.

Even McDonald's has a fascinating story. Whatever you want to say about McDonald's, their model and the way they work with their suppliers and what they did, it's fascinating. The Mondavi story, their wineries, I mean I can go on. I read these autobiographies, but not one is a business book. I've never read a technical business book. It would be wasted on me. Honestly. I couldn't get through it, I know it.

**Tracey:**  Could you describe a typical working day for you?

**Craig:** It depends how late I'm up with the factory overseas. I get up. I just check whatever messages there are, tons of emails. I start sorting through them, media request, orders, this, that and the other thing. It's then just phone calls coming in. I talk to my artist usually a few times during the day. We're usually involved with a few custom jobs that we're on a deadline. We're always on a deadline. There's always something.

I told you we're starting this new division with our Canardgrams. We were just ducks, but now.... So now my day is about what's happening with the printing of the chocolate boxes, how's chocolate production, the soap manufacturer needs the money wired out, building new websites for the new divisions. There is just so many little things hovering all the time.

I have this humongous company and multiple divisions, with one person - it's so bizarre. It still cracks me up. I still remember when I was doing Coke and at one point there was a Coke commercial that they did with the NBA. So there's the NBA players, all animated. We were doing a scene from the commercial.

So Coke called me one morning, I'm shaving. I'm naked, I'm shaving. They said, 'Okay, we've got the NBA on the phone, so we're going to work a dual licence contract for you to do that art piece.' So the NBA's on, Coke, and me—naked with shaving cream on my face—working out the details of the contract. Which we did, no big deal. I just didn't mention it to them because it was hard to get everyone together. So really, here we all were, we've got to just move with the moment.

I do a lot of interviews. I usually do one or two interviews a week, either by radio or in person. Someone wanted me to write a business blog. They said I'd be the perfect for marketing to do it because of my story. I wrote back and said, 'Look, I'm flattered, but do you really want me as your business guy? Someone who doesn't understand technically business? I don't think you'd want me.' But actually, he did. He said, 'Actually you're the type of person we do want, who is not just conventional business, kind of more street-savvy. But I still thanked him, I said, 'No.'

You know what that was? Mainly time constraints. If the day was forty-eight hours and not twenty-four, I still couldn't fit it all in. I think I told you I had a little music studio. I'm working on an album. I swear I just wish I could just devote all my time to that at the same time there's books I'm reading. I'm reading history. This new book came out on the history of Walt Disney, it's like this thick. I'm just loving it. Plus I like to read my Buddhist books. There's no shortage of things for me to do. I mean people say to me sometimes, they go, 'I'm bored.' I don't know what I'd do if I had extra time. Give me your hours.

**Tracey:** If you had to start over, would you do anything differently?

**Craig:** Yeah, I probably would. In the beginning you have to be cautious with your resources. Some licences, probably wouldn't have paid as much as I did for them. Certain ones I wouldn't have paid for. Certain ones I wouldn't have done. Certain ones that I should have gone after that would have been more money. It would have been worth doing it because they would have sold better. It would have been such a strong brand statement.

Sometimes you have to make strategic decisions for what's best for the brand. Even though they cost more money, that's money well spent. Even though you'd probably be conservative in areas, there's a time to be conservative, there's times where it's better to be expansive. You have to get a feel for when it does make sense to spend the money and when it doesn't.

It's like I told you, with the Bob Marley people. Look, I like Bob Marley, three thousand to five thousand dollar advance, fine. But we're talking fifty thousand dollars for Bob Marley advance against sales. That to me is not sensitive to this economy, the timing's not right. Yes, if some huge chain says we want to put thousands of Bob Marley ducks in, fine, but that hasn't happened. What you notice a lot of times in licensing, a lot of people, not the best ones, they want a lot of money for them. It's sometimes a one-sided thing.

Here's another thing I would say to any entrepreneur about the way that I do business. I'm a pretty good negotiator, but the only negotiation that works for me is the one that we both feel good at the end of it. I could push people harder and probably get a little bit more for me, but then I lose too. So I don't do that.

When I was negotiating with my box manufacturer, at a certain point I was trying to work it out for the chocolate box, for the candies and make the price points work. I could tell she really hit the bottom and said, 'End of conversation. That's the price.' That's fair. That was a real price that works for her, that works for me.

What I was getting to, is you notice a lot of times in corporations, when they do deals, it's to get as much money as they can for themselves and they don't really take a look at what's best for that person. How much money they can get and hopefully you'll make a lot of money for them. That is not a good business model. Just in the psychophysics of the universe, that's not a good business model. You should want to see that you don't do anything that jeopardises the people you're working with or puts them in a tough spot.

So yes, Mr. Bob Marley licensor, I may give you fifty thousand dollars over time, based on sales, but let's pay that based on royalties on sales, not just give you a chunk of money up front and then if it doesn't pan out, I could be really screwed. One of the biggest things to me is just learning—learning where to spend money and where not to spend money.

I'll tell you another mistake a lot of people make. They've got the business, they get their offices, they got their new computers, their printers, their this, that and the other thing. You know what? You don't need all that to begin with. What you need is a tiny little room in your house. Today with the Internet, your website, you could look like Walmart but be sitting in a trailer. Work on the things that really count, the product, your image, your website. Don't worry about all the little top technical things and huge office and huge overhead and huge staff.

People, a lot of times, they get venture capital and they spend it really stupidly. I hate to say, because it's given to them. If you talk to the entrepreneurs, more like myself or like people you've spoken to, where's the  money come from? Family. They are a lot more cautious with that money.

You can call me conservative and I even say to people, 'Yeah, I probably do run my business more like Grandma Moses'. But we're here, we'll always be here. The economy can go upside down. What did Cher say? She said, at the end of the nuclear holocaust there'll be two things left: the cockroaches and her.

And CelebriDucks. Because we're not leveraging any way that could destroy us. You always want to run your business to think what if anything went wrong.

Another thing entrepreneurs do, they get a big order from this company. Do you know that's like a blessing and a curse? If you ever leverage with one company, their interest isn't always your company. If the product has any flaw or anything goes wrong or doesn't sell, they can send it back. You can go under. They can put you under very quickly. Don't get all excited.

Buddhists have a point of view. They don't get too excited about anything. You don't get too depressed about anything. Just enjoy life and be intelligent and don't get wrapped up in any one big thing because that could take away all your time and prevent your growth and actually could end up hurting you if it turns sour. Diversify.

For me, I'm a big believer in outsourcing to the best people because then, if things do change, you're not carrying the overhead. I always tell people when I do these business interviews, do you remember those big brands that are just not in the US anymore? There's millions of them, the landscape is littered with them. They're not here today. They were making millions, multimillions, billions in some cases. They're not here.

Overheads will kill you. It's not how much money you make. You've got to pump this into these entrepreneur's heads. They're always, 'How much am I going to make'. It's not how much money you make, it's how much you keep. Don't forget that. Use your resources wisely. You don't have to look important and tell people you make billions and millions. Grow your brand intelligently. That day will come, or not, but you'll create a foundation. Lay the foundation.

How many people who have these ideas, then spend tons of money and it's just not been tested. They didn't test the concept. You could say I didn't test CelebriDucks either, but I had Name that Toon, my animation company. I had a base.

Don't be spending money stupidly without a base. That was money I could afford to lose. I felt the duck was a calculated risk. It worked. A couple of ducks - that to me is a calculated risk. The risks that aren't calculated, where you just spend money, dollar after dollar and if you lose it you're out of business, that's not a calculated risk, that's stupid.

**Tracey:** You've had lots of media coverage, did you specifically go out after the media coverage or did it sort of come your way?

**Craig:** Both. We do send out press releases. There's people from media looking for stories. Every day I send out things to people who might want to do a story about us. Then I send out press releases if we have something big happening, like maybe with the launch of the green duck. First-ever recycled green duck. For big things, we'll do a press release.

At a certain point it kind of feeds on itself. All of a sudden some celebrity or someone is on TV with your duck or some magazine has one or they see it. My daughter comes over the other day. She goes, 'Oh, my ex-mother-in-law, I love her, she's great. She was watching *Who Wants to be a Millionaire*. One of the questions was according to the friend, 'CelebriDucks is a company that makes rubber ducks of celebrities. What famous rubber ducky did they make who carries numchucks - Bruce Lee, Woody Allen, Humphrey Bogart or James Dean? And the guy on the show goes, 'Bruce Lee'. He goes, 'Correct for $500.'

So you see, bit by bit you become part of the cultural landscape. With CelebriDucks, the more we do, the more we sell. Every box is an advertisement, every store that sells one, they find out about us. It just keeps growing and growing and growing and then people find us.

I'd say 50 percent of the people contact us, we didn't need to reach out to. They were in stores or through media and they heard about it. We think Top 100 *Entertainment Weekly*, the *Tonight Show*, we think we're legends in our own mind. Well those people really don't know us in the greater scheme of things.

When people say, what do you do? It's 'Oh really?' Then they go to the website 'whoa'. They don't know we exist. We've done hundreds of thousands of them. We sell them all over the world, but we haven't broken through. We will. We definitely will. There's no question in my mind.

If we were Hasbro or Mattel and had their money behind us, we'd be a worldwide brand everywhere, you'd know us immediately. But we're not Hasbro or Mattel and they haven't called to buy us. So I run it my own way.

Yes, if I took my money and got loans and venture capital, I could do it and we'd be all over the place. Everyone has their own style. I was never willing to give up the business. If someone wanted to buy it lock, stock and barrel, fine. I don't think I'm one of these people who wants to have investors.

There's a TV show called *Shark Tank* in the US. You go before these big investors and you say 'I have this business, would you like to invest in it?' Then they give you money and they take control of your business or a big chunk of it. I'd like to get on that show. They probably wouldn't invest in it, because, I mean, we have supermarket chains who said if you develop a point of purchase display, we'll put it in supermarkets across the country. It's a big investment in money and time. I haven't been willing to do it. But if you had the venture capital and people to do it and could hire a national salesman, yeah we could do it.

The other thing I tell entrepreneurs, be careful what you wish for. Who said it? I don't know but 'Know thyself, to thyself be true.' Really know who you are. I'm not Donald Trump. I'm me. And run it within who you are, in the confines of what works for you.

What makes it fun? If you want to take it to the next level and you find people you can work with and you feel good about it and that works for you, great. If there's other people who come to me one day and I feel really comfortable with them, fine. But until that happens, I guess I just run it the way I run it. It's what I know.

**Tracey:** So where to from here? What's the next step?

**Craig:** Well, now there are these Canardgrams and Greengrams which are opening up a whole new thing for us. So we're expanding into a whole cosmetic line, the soap's only the first. Then with this chocolate, yes, the start is the chocolate ducks, but there's a whole bunch of stuff we can expand into from there.

Then we're going to set up a whole division, eventually when we get big enough, to do licensing and licence our brand. Just like Coke does. So you can get a CocoCanard T-shirt. You see, another company would do a whole CocoCanard line of apparel. You can see where it's going and they would licence it and we'd be the licensor licensing the image. That's my ultimate goal is to really develop the brand to that point where people license CelebriDucks. To maximise distribution. We've only touched the potential. I feel we're like one one-thousandth of the potential of this company and I don't know if we're even there yet.

Almost every college in the country would love us to do their mascot. Do you know how many colleges there are? No one's ever not wanted a mascot, they look great. The alumni love them. The students love them. They're the most unique, fun product. But then we have to set up distribution with national sales manager, with sales representatives and that takes time. It'll happen. That in itself would be a whole division, just the college market.

One of the biggest sports in the United States is NASCAR. Yeah, cars running round a track, it's huge. These drivers are like gods, they're amazing. We should be in NASCAR. We did some and they sold right out. We should get NASCAR licence with the top drivers and we should be getting the whole NASCAR distribution up. It's a whole other business.

There's all these little pockets, just like I do the Blues Brothers for all the House of Blues around the country. I did the pink flamingo. No one had ever done a floating pink flamingo. We did that for the Flamingo Hotel in Vegas. There's these niches. Just like Coke.

I'm doing the same thing I always did back with Coke. I go for niches. And everybody wants to be everything to everybody, but I tell entrepreneurs, you don't need to be everything to all people, because then you lose your identity. Just own your niche. Be the best in your niche.

I feel we are probably one of the best duck companies in the world and nobody does what we do as far as this goes. But there's a million niches. There was the Budweiser niche —no one thought about these people. Everything's Disney, Warner Brothers. No one thought about all these shows on *Home Shopping Network.* We do fifty thousand dollars in one night just with Budweiser collectors, with our Budweiser sales.

There's a million other niches to be found and to be mined. I can't even tell you how many ideas and new niches that we're going to be getting into. There's people who just love their dogs. We could just get into that market with dog CelebriDucks and you'd have a huge market. How many people love their terriers like Toto? It's huge.

Every niche has hundreds of thousands of millions of people. Do the math. How many niches and you can see we're talking multi, multi, multimillion dollars. What's stopping it? Well, you could say me. I'm not really stopping it. It's just that I haven't been willing to borrow to do it. Maybe that would be fine for some people. They have the temperament to get into deep debt and leverage and I respect those people. I'm not saying they shouldn't do it.

Again, know what you can live with. I'm not one of those people who does well with debt. I just don't sleep well at night. It's just who I am. It takes everything from me not just to pay off the final payments on the mortgage. My accountant is, 'Don't do it, just wait.' I just want to pay it off. It's just the way I'm wired. If some other big company came in and took over CelebriDucks and put the money into it? *Vroom,* they'd be making multimillion dollars immediately, niches are there. They're there to be had. I'm happy and we'll get there.

**Tracey:** I read somewhere that CelebriDucks were voted the number one novelty item?

**Craig:** Yeah. It was really interesting. There are all these other collectibles out there, Matchbox cars, Beanie babies, lunchboxes, tin lunchboxes with characters on them. Then ESPN did this poll from the fans, just a little poll. Which would you rather see as a giveaway at a game promotion. There were these big brands like Matchbox cars and Beanie babies. People said CelebriDucks. We actually won the poll.

**Tracey:** So is there anything more that you'd like to add that I might not have covered before we go? Any last words of wisdom?

**Craig:** I don't know what else I could say except the way I started was with what I was passionate about and this is something I told my daughter when she was young. We lived in Los Angeles at the time and she was young. She was growing up there and a lot of attention is on sex and drugs. You can't suppress that, I'm not even suggesting it, but I was always trying to suss out what really turned her on. Sex and drugs is something people do, but it's not necessarily something from the heart. It is maybe in a relationship, otherwise it's nothing from the heart.

The deeper things are what really inspire you to live a life, not just something that turns you on. It's not about you, it's bigger. I know she really loved art and so when I started Name that Toon, she was another of my inspirations for the Disney drawings. I noticed how much she loved doing it. It gravitated, it just brought her into a whole other place, she came alive with it. So anything to do with art really inspires her.

Then years later, she did a product design major, went to college and she designed all the ducks in the early days. She ended up working for Pottery Barn, a big chain in the US and Hello Kitty. She worked for them and she became a very good designer and the stuff she did for me is still some of my best stuff.

I said to her, 'I don't know how much money you'll make with your art, but if you really feel passionate about it, do it, because the way I look at it, whatever money you make, at least you wake up every day you'll be happy.

As far as I can tell something like 90 percent of people are in jobs are not really fully enjoying it and money comes around and they're kind of not digging it. So pick something that you feel passionate about. Seems for you, it's art.' And that's what she did. So that's my closing words, follow thy passion.

## *After the interview . . .*

What happened after the interview is a whole story in itself. Craig and I went to his office and he 'introduced' me to all of the ducks. They are unreal.

Craig loves what he does and is passionate about his product and his company. I imagine there are many people who would give Craig a lot of 'cheek' about his ducks. I know many people ask, 'Do you really make a living with rubber ducks in the likeness of a celebrity?' But Craig has proven that passion will win out every time.

Imagine if you could have just 10 percent of the passion Craig has, but in and for *your* business? After meeting him face-to-face, I'd say you would be rocketing to success.

The other thing that Craig talked about that resonated with me was his negotiation style. He is looking for a win-win solution. I believe that through negotiation you can really see a person's character. It is the quality of your character that is so vital to the success of your business and your life for that matter. If like Craig, you work, negotiate and play for a win-win outcome and do so with true compassion for the other person or company, how can you ever go wrong?

What a fascinating story of an unusual product and a man with true passion for what he does.

Thanks Craig.

For more information about Craig, check out:

www.celebriducks.com

*Introducing . . .*

# Paul Mann

In giving you people who made their millions in different home-based businesses, I knew I needed to include an entrepreneur who had successfully franchised their business. The challenge with this is that I discovered some franchisors, when they sell their franchises, they don't really care about whether their franchisees are successful or not.

With Paul, I hit the jackpot. Not only does he have a franchise where both he and his franchisees are home-based business owners, Paul also cares about them, about their business and wants to help them succeed. His business does not finish after the sale of the franchise.

You will see and feel this integrity in his words. I hope you enjoy and learn from my chat with Paul.

## *Interview with Paul Mann . . .*

**Tracey:** How about if we just start with you telling us a little about your story?

**Paul:** Well my story starts with, I went to college and I studied engineering in upstate New York. I came out of there, worked for companies like Estee Lauder and IBM and my job was what was called systems process re-engineering, which is looking at an operation and streamlining it and making it as efficient as possible. I did that.

After that I went to work for my father's company. My father invented the sterile ear-piercing system back in the mid 1970s that became world famous. I worked for him and again did systems process re-engineering. His dad was a paper delivery guy, that's what he did for his work, so my dad kind of took it upon himself to come up with a unique idea.

He really was passionate about design, industrial design and that's what he did, he studied it in college. From there he worked and was just very meticulous about learning all he could and about working for companies designing products until he felt he was ready. He went and he looked for a product that he could own. He just looked at something, at a process of ear piercing, which then was done with mostly needles. He said, 'I could do that better and I have a design that I can do'.

I watched someone like him take a very simple concept that was not working well and improve on it. Of course, it became a multimillion dollar company and he owned the market share by the time he retired. I went to work for him for a few years and then realised I couldn't work for the family business. I left, but picked up a lot of great experience there and at IBM and Estee Lauder.

I helped start a high-tech job placement firm in the early 1990s in New York. I am not good at taking something that's already been done and doing it also. If you ask me to open an insurance company or a travel agency or whatever, I'll be competitive, but I'm not really going to excel. So I knew I had to do something different.

When we started our job placement firm we were one of the first companies to use resume matching software that would allow us to match-up a candidate faster. We also got technology professionals in to place technology professionals into the jobs. We did very well. We opened twenty-nine locations nationwide and sold the company to a multinational in 1996.

At that time, it was the middle of the dot-com era. I moved out here to California and again I said 'What can I do differently?' Online survey technology was something we learned about. A lot of people were taking paper based surveys and again we said, 'What can we do differently with that?' We came out with an online survey technology and we made it very unique and very robust. By 2001, we had almost half the Fortune 500 companies using it to gather feedback from their customers.

I was CEO, we were doing very well and I was miserable. I had my BMW, we were in an air-conditioned beautiful building, but I thought to myself 'Where is my life going here?' I decided to sell my business and take some time off.

I was going to take a year off, working on the house that I had just bought. As I was taking measurements for the house, before I took ownership, this woman came in and took out the dog of the current owner and when she came back I said 'Are you a friend of the owner?' She said, 'No, I'm a dog walker.'

I had never heard of a dog walker before. I said, 'What do you get paid?' And she said, 'I get paid twenty dollars.' I said, 'Twenty dollars for twenty minutes, that's phenomenal.' She said, 'Well that's nothing. Bill, down the hill here, he takes out three groups of six dogs a day.' I did the math and I realised Bill grossed over one hundred thousand US dollars a year and I thought, 'I'll never look at a pet sitter the same way.'

I obviously didn't go from CEO to being a dog walker, so I put that away, but then later that year I was looking for a pet sitter for my pets and I couldn't find anyone. I called everyone in the phone book. Everyone was either booked up or they didn't cover my area, or I just didn't feel comfortable. That's when I got what I call the 'Aha moment'.

It's like 'Aha, wait a minute.' Two-thirds of all households in America have pets, one or more pets. There is a lack of professionally trained operators, and it was a forty—well right now it's forty-five—billion dollar industry. The pet industry will be fifty-two billion next year and it's the seventh largest in the US, the seventh largest retail industry, ahead of retail jewellery, toy, candy, and hardware industries. It's the sixth fastest industry, right behind consumer electronics—that'd be computers and phones and all those things that we have to have.

I thought to myself, 'Okay, the issue is if I go out and I try to be a dog walker I'll be just another dog walker. There's eight thousand of those folks, maybe more. What I need to do is something unique.'

I took my background again, and that's the key thing. I said, well, two things. Number one, 'Was I passionate about it?' Of course. I grew up with pets, I love pets. Second thing is, 'Could I add some value to the business?' That's where I took my background and said, 'Wait a minute, I really understand systems process re-engineering, how to streamline a business.'

So I automated the whole back office operations. Billing, payroll, marketing, all the things that need to happen on the background I automated with internet-based software, because I understood that. Then I put a large staff on the front end and we took on the name 'Fetch Pet Care' and our tagline is 'We've got your tail covered.'

**Tracey:** That's really good.

**Paul:** Yeah, and what that means is that whenever, wherever, someone needs us, we have it covered. It means a lot of things, but that's primarily what it means for me. So the idea then is you start building staff.

Within one year I had built up over seventy sitters, that's seven zero. Seventy sitters on staff, three dispatchers answering my phones and I was servicing over one thousand customers. That's when I said, 'Okay, I think I'm doing this right. I'm the number one provider here in the US, here in San Francisco, inside of a year. Now let's franchise it.'

The next thing was to say, 'How do I take my model and build it out nationwide?' That's what we did. Today we have over 230 franchisees providing service in 1800 cities and towns in 39 states and we have over 5000 pet sitters on staff. We're partnered up with great corporations like AAA, PetCo and Google who are promoting us to their customers, their employees and their members. So we're really seeing just tremendous growth. We're getting written up everywhere. We're on TV. I was on NPR, National Public Radio, recently. I was on many, many radio, many TV, many media stations where we were building the brand.

If I look at the business, this is the most exciting thing I've ever done. It's exciting for a lot of reasons. First of all, we're helping pets. Our vision, our mission, is that all pets should be cared for. We are also employing lots of people. We are helping franchisees realise their dream of being business owners. We're having a lot of fun. We get to be goofy.

For me, it's always a unique day. It's always exciting. I'm always passionate about this. I think that if you were to start a business, the key things that I think any new business owner wants to look for, is first of all they want to ask themselves what's in their core, what is really important to them, their values.

When I go back to the last company I was at, the internet survey company. It was fun, but my goal in life was not to be the survey king. I enjoyed helping corporations make more money, but that wasn't really fulfilling for me. When I work with pets or when I work with children or when I help people, now that, that's huge for me, that's at the core of my values.

When I have that, I have two things. I have passion and I have commitment and I have, I guess three, drive. Every day I am just absolutely committed and driven to do more in this business. The second thing I look for 'Does this really resonate well to business for me? Is it a business opportunity?' That's where we look at the market and if somebody else is doing this already, hey, that might be a good thing. If you can do it better, if you can look at their business process and improve on it. That's what the Japanese call *kaizen*, constant improvement, then that's an opportunity.

I looked at this business on a few levels. I looked at market opportunity, the fact that it was a highly unserviced business category. There weren't many professional providers in the category. Second thing is, I looked at was who are the customers? The customers, a lot of them are the baby boomers. They have the projected income for the next decade or two, so I knew it was a stable business.

By the way, our business has been recession resistant. We've actually been increasing our sales. We're probably going to do almost 200 percent growth this year over last year.

So you want to look at, does the customer base support it? Not just is there a demand, but are they going to buy it? You might have the greatest idea, but do they really need it? Do they really have the expendable income for that? When I looked at my customer base, I realised the answer was yes to those questions. Then the third thing, I looked at what can I personally contribute to this. What are my skill sets, my core capabilities?

I didn't do all this at the outset, but if I could do it again, I'd look even harder at what are my core capabilities and only do those. The things that I'm not good at, hire other people to do it, outsource it, partner, whatever you need to do, but find other people to assist you in building your vision.

An example is I understand programming but I'm not a programmer. So right away I got a programmer. Right now in my business, I can do the accounting, but now I'm giving away all the accounting and the human resources to someone else because it's not a good use of my time.

So know what you're good at, focus on what you're good at because it's basically opportunity cost. If you're doing one thing, it takes you away from doing another thing. I think a lot of us focus on the little tasks that we can all do, 'Oh, I'll just take care of this little thing.' I recommend, take on the big things that really matter. The little things don't matter as much and if you don't focus on those and maybe either give those other tasks to someone else or do them later, you'll accelerate in your business. You'll be much more effective as a business owner.

It's a very competitive market place, whatever business you go into today, so you have to be like a skilled athlete. You have to have a lot of focus, a lot of dedication and training, and really, you have to be diligent. So to kind of do something well is not a recipe for long-term success.

Understand your strengths and weaknesses and be real about those and I think also have a good time. You know, so many people, they get so serious about their work and their intent to make money. I don't think it's about making money. My dad always said, 'If you do what you love, you'll love what you do and the money will come.' I really believe it.

I think that we're given these gifts if we do the right thing. We all have some sort of mission, why we're here. I think we must. If you focus on that, what really is that divine inspiration for you that makes a difference in your day? Go do that and then you'll be taken care of financially, all the things that you need will come. It's about focused attention on doing one thing really well.

A lot of people try, they have a lot of ideas and they try to spread themselves really wide with a lot of these. 'Hey, it would be great if they launched with a new computer system and we could come out with five different product lines and we could go sell this worldwide.' Don't try to do that, try to come out with a simple solution. Don't build your own software if you don't have to, if it already exists, for example. Come out with one product. Do that really well. Sell it locally, then build it out geographically and then come out with more products. You have to work very systematically and stay focused.

If I look at my business, all the time we get opportunities for us to sell other things and to go into other product lines and do other things. There are so many areas that we could go into, other services, and I keep bringing it back to what is our core?

If I look back at my Dad's business, he had a very successful health and beauty aids company. He did the ear piercing systems, but he had a whole other line of other products, waxing and depilatories and hair removal products, all kinds of female products.

I remember, at a young age, I even said to him, 'I don't think you should do all those things, I think if you focus on one thing, ear piercing and just do that as well as you can, you will have global domination.' He didn't agree, he wanted to come out with a lot of lines.

He did very well, but today he's not the largest provider of ear piercing. There's another company that came out and another company that came out and they did it better, more efficiently and that's all that they did. So today, his market share has dwindled. It's not to say that it's still not good and it's doing well, his former company is doing well, but what if he had really focused on one thing and absolutely owned that? What could he have done with that?

That's sort of my lesson that I'm trying to bring into my company. We've had tremendous growth and acceleration, but we also have tremendous focus. I can tell everyone in my company, from the corporate level all the way down to the person who's doing the dog walking, what our mission and vision is. It's very focused and everybody gets it and they can recite it. You want to have that sort of clarity in your business. Again, if you try to do too many things, you'll be spread thin and you won't realise the accelerated growth that maybe you'd like to have.

**Tracey:** Has there ever been a time that you doubted yourself or what you were doing?

**Paul:** Of course. I think fear and doubt come in all the time. It's actually an okay thing to question 'Is this the right thing to be doing?' People ask me 'Hey, Paul, weren't you afraid to go to your next venture when you were already a CEO of another company?' I said, 'Yeah, I was of course terrified.'

But I was more scared of staying where I was, than going forward because I knew intuitively, internally, this was not where I wanted to be anymore, or where I wanted to go. I was driven by passion and it felt like the right thing.

I think that's part of entrepreneurship, you have to listen to your intuition. Intuition is a gift. We all have it. I think the people who really excel as entrepreneurs are people who really understand how to use it. If you don't take chances, you're going to be that insurance company next door that competes with everyone else. If you're willing to take some chances, you'll have some failures. I've had failures, but overall I've had wins, so they're calculated failures.

I always question what I do. I think that's a good thing. If you don't question or have fear or doubt about what you're doing, find someone who does, because that allows you to test it. I think my family were my greatest critics. I remember when I wanted to start this business my Dad said, 'You're going to be a dog walker?' 'No, no, you don't get it. I'm going to sell this nationwide.' He didn't see it and that was okay. I didn't need his approval, but I needed to hear where he had issues so that I could address those internally and be a stronger company. I think it's always good.

If you're not self-doubting in some way, find someone who is. But at some point you have to turn that off. You have to have rationale and be able to see both sides and say, 'Okay, I'm freaking out right now about this issue in my business. Where is this coming from? Is this a real issue or is this something that I've based on something historic that's happened to me?'

A lot of us have been told in our lives—and this is a big thing for entrepreneurs to get, for anyone who wants to start a business—a lot of us have read or we've been told that we can't achieve whatever we want. Most people listen to that and they believe they can't do it.

They're going to be stuck in that realm of awareness or lack of awareness. A realm of being, actually, that's the world that they live in. It's a world of doubt and fear. It's unfortunate and most people have been fed that propaganda by their family or by themselves in some way.

The real exciting part is breaking out of that and saying, 'I get it. I'm totally freaking out now about this issue and I'm going to search now and figure out where is that coming from. Is it from something I read? Is it from my family? Is it from self-doubt? What is it?' Get to the core of it and then take it on.

I think one cool thing about business is, yeah it's cool to make lots of money and that's fine, but I think the exciting part about business is what do you do when you come up against obstacles and challenges. How do you take that and how are you going to deal with it? I deal with this every day. This is not easy running a business. That's why they call it business. You're going to get problems and issues every day and I've learned to come at it from a point of strength rather than fear. A point of calm rather than panic.

When you start a business, there's a lot of fear and panic. A lot of breathing is required. Get a good base of friends or supporters who will support you when you need to talk to someone. It's always good to have a coach of some sort or an ear who can just play things back to you. Because it's going to happen, you're going to have feelings of fear and doubt. Don't let it get you down, look at it instead as a challenge.

I come up with challenges every day about how we going to achieve this grand vision that I have, that I'm holding in my head. I look at it as a puzzle, not as an impossible wall or road block. That to me is exciting, it becomes a game. Business is a game and it's really about getting geeked by it, getting excited by it and saying, 'Okay, we've got a little challenge here. What are we going to do? How are we going to take this on?' Not giving up, but how are we going to do it? If you have that belief, you will do it.

**Tracey:** A lot of things you've said totally resonate with me. I always say to people, don't look for the money, look for where you can add value, but as a master franchisor, what's the biggest thing you see is your role with your many franchisees? How do you add the most amount of value to your franchisees?

**Paul:** I look at myself as the strategist for the business. I'm constantly looking at putting myself in their shoes and saying 'What do they need to be absolutely successful?' I'm kind of like an investment advisor for them. Okay, so they've given me their money, their franchise fee. It's my job to make sure that I do the best with it that I can, to maximise the return on their investment.

That's my job, to increase their return on investment—make them a lot of money. I'm always looking at, do they need new software systems? Do we need more public relations coverage? Do we need more marketing? Do we need more partnerships? What do we need? What do they need? Do they need more marketing materials? I'm constantly looking at that and then I'm also there to be with them and say 'Tell me what you're thinking about. It's not just what I think, but what do you want to achieve as a business? What are your challenges? What do you see as the opportunities?'

An example is recently in Arizona, where it's very hot, like I'm talking 125 degrees Fahrenheit on some days—scorching temperatures. A franchisee came to me and she said 'We have a problem. It's so hot we can't do group dog exercise, we can't let the dogs go out and run or walk after nine thirty in the morning and we can't take them out again until about six or seven o'clock at night. It's just too hot. We want to and the customers want us to, because they need that to occur during the day while they're at work so that we can get the angst out so that the dogs don't chew up the house and they're tired when the owner comes home.

So we put it together and I said, 'Hmm, hot, we're a home business. What about this? Let's rent a bunch of trailers from U-Haul, let's put some air conditioners in, let's put some treadmills in and let's let them run in an air conditioned space, mobile, brought to your home.' Now they're looking at that opportunity as just not even buying the trailers, just renting them. You could even rent the treadmills and the fans, rent it all and go home-to-home just offering the service.

There's an example of innovation. Taking a challenge and a problem and coming up with something that's super exciting, that never existed before. That's what I get excited by, how you create something of value that's never existed? It's called innovation.

If you're just doing something that's already done, well that's great, your helping, but you're not really satisfying a greater purpose. To me, I like to stimulate people's minds, because I think if I can get them to think at a higher level, their game is going to be at a higher level. We're going to raise the bar. They're going to make someone else's game play at a higher level. What I do with one franchisee might pay forward to three hundred people that they know, who knows somebody, who knows somebody. That's what I'm always trying to do, how I can add value.

**Tracey:** That's fantastic. So what do you think the biggest skill you've had to develop and learn over this time has been?

**Paul:** Patience. When you first start a business you have these grand visions? I know I do. I can see where this, and whatever business I've been in, where I want it to go and then I take it even beyond that. I get really excited by that. That's the mandala I hold in my mind, where our company is going to go, it keeps me focused.

The problem around that is wanting to do too much, too fast and then what happens is we burn our employees out and we don't meet our goals. Customers or partners are let down, employees are let down.

It's really having patience and diligence to create a solid plan and execute it in that step-by-step manner. If you looked at 'Here I am at starting date, I haven't yet started my business and here's where I want to be when I grow up. Here's where I want my business to be.' Create a plan that gets you from here to here and execute on that one step at a time, systematically. Don't jump ahead, but do it one step at a time. Then measure your success and don't go forward until you have measured growth before you accelerate to the next step.

**Tracey:** You did mention earlier that you had a few family members that may have doubted you. Was there anyone else out there that doubted you and how did you deal with that? Doubted what you were going to do and the vision for the business?

**Paul:** I had a handful of people that I played my idea to and my Dad is my consummate doubter. Pokes holes in things. My Mum is my consummate cheerleader. 'You can do it, whatever it is, you can do it.' You kind of have to know who you're dealing with. You have to know what you can expect from them. Then if you hear something totally different, wow, now that's something you want to listen to. But if it's the same story again it's like 'okay, this is what he always does' or 'this is what she always does.' So you have to be careful about who you go to and what sort of feedback you absorb.

I took that feedback from my parents because I knew. Yeah, that's good and they have some good insights, but I also knew that I needed to get other people to really get the rounded feedback that I needed.

Now, again, part of this is, I don't know if it's that I have tremendous confidence or I'm just insanely stubborn, but if I'm passionate about something I'm going to do it. I'm going to go for it unless you can prove to me it's absolutely ridiculous. If I can see it, I can envision it.

It goes back to the fact it's not about always making millions of dollars, it's about the journey. It's about that ride of building something, or trying to build something, and seeing if it can be done. I've had my failures, but as you do more and more of these things you kind of hone your skills and you learn what's realistic and what's not and so the likelihood of failure becomes less. As my game gets bigger, I also go to people who are bigger in terms of what they have achieved.

I am in the CEO's group and we meet every month and it's a group of about a dozen CEOs here in the San Francisco Bay area and they're my peers. Some of them are small in business size, some of them are monstrous and I listen more to the monstrous ones in terms of where I might be going, but I also listen very much to the smaller ones, because they're having wins or they're making mistakes that I can learn from. I very much value everyone's feedback, but I also keep it in perspective at a certain point.

**Tracey:** If someone came up to you and said, 'Hey, you know, what you've done is fantastic but I could never do what you've done', what would you say to them?

**Paul:** Probably not, you know, if that's their take on it. It's almost a self-defeating attitude. I'd ask the question, 'Why don't you think you could do it? What makes you think you couldn't achieve something?' I'd look hard at that and I'd look at the core of that, because a lot of that might stem from disbelief that's been created from a very young age. If I had time to sit with that person, I could probably pinpoint exactly at a younger age where they decided that they couldn't be in that game.

Most of us have, unfortunately, if you look at the shaping of our lives, most of the trauma occurs at a young age when we didn't understand, when something happened and we created a story around it. Not the reality of what actually happened, but when little Bobby didn't want to play with us, we didn't get that he actually didn't sleep that night before, so he just wanted to sit down and play in the sandbox by himself. Instead, we took it on that 'he doesn't like me.'

If we could rationalise and understand those things that occurred, like when someone told you 'you'll never be president' or whatever it may be, whoever said that, that is their opinion but that has no outcome on what you could actually achieve your own potential.

I would have them go back and 'check the code' and figure out where that occurred in your life and then change it. You need to recognise where your point of self-defeat is, take it on and then re-script it, change your life. Why can't you be? What do you want out of your life? I'd go back to say 'What do you really want in your life?'

See some people don't want to be. My wife doesn't want to be a millionaire. She's not wired that way. If she goes into her core, her core is that she's all about truth, about fairness, about information and being educated. So for her, that's what she's seeking in her life, so she could not run my business if she came to me. But what she's achieving in her life is huge, because she's actuated those three things in her life.

I'd ask that person to go back and say 'Go and consult yourself on what's really important to you and then if there's something that's in the way, look at why it's there, knock it out of the way like a tennis ball with a racquet. Just knock it out and focus on turning that voice off and focus on being empowered and confident to achieve those goals.'

**Tracey:** Is there anything that you do on a regular basis that helps you be successful? Is there anything that you put into your routine?

**Paul:** Yeah, absolutely. First of all, I approach business holistically and what success means for me is not just 'Hey, let's look at our P&L. Are we making money today?' I look at what's important for me overall, and the business. For me personally, when I look back at my life ten or thirty years from now, what do I want to look back and see? I asked myself that very early on. How do I measure success? Success for me would be having spent a lot of time with my family, getting lots of exercise and being able to travel and be financially secure.

Every day I work from home. My business is purposely designed so that I can be at home every day. I've been with my four-year-old son every day since he was born, with the exception of when I had to travel a very few times, I purposely don't travel much. I don't do a lot of media tours. I have other people go do those, because to me, being with my family, my wife, our sons, that's what's important.

The second part is exercise. I try to swim as much as I can. I dance two to three nights a week, often times with my wife. The last part is travel, so I built it in where we travel. We spent a month and a half in the South of France in a home exchange. Now how do I do that? Voice over IP and internet access where I could work, where we were in the mountains for a week, eleven days, without internet access because I built a great team.

That's how I measure success. Am I happy? Are my employees happy? Are my customers happy? Are my partners happy? It's the bigger picture and so it's about my personal happiness, but do I need to reach out to my employees? Do we need to have a picnic? Do we need to reach out to our partners and thank them? There's a lot of things that go into a business and a business is a living organism. So is it functioning, is it healthy, are the people, everyone involved, healthy? That's how I measure success.

A lot of businesses, too many corporations today, go to eke out profits at the expense of people and the environment and it's horrible what's going on. Unfortunately, more companies than you would imagine are doing this and we are just draining the life out of people and the environment as a result. It's not good.

So it has to be sustainable. Business has to be sustainable. It has to be fun for everyone. Why are we here? Why are we doing this? If it's not fun, if we're not making a positive impact on many fronts in the world, then it's 'Go find something else.' I mean that's the new realm to me. That's the exciting part of today.

When I look back at the dot-com era I thought 'Wow, it will never be like this again.' When I looked at the pet industry, I was amazed at how much there is in opportunity. When I look now at this whole thing with social media, this blows away anything that's ever happened before. When I look at this whole green movement, it's amazing. There is so much opportunity and I think opportunity is right under everyone's noses. If everyone just takes a look at 'How can I really add value to something that I'm passionate about?' you'll come up with a hundred ideas. Just sit down and make some time to do that.

That's the other problem, people don't sit down and take the time to think about their future and say 'Okay, if I want to start a business, what am I really passionate about? What could I do? Where is there something missing? What can be improved on?' Don't try to invent something new if it doesn't really come to you, if that's not your inclination. Just look at something that's already being done and look if there's a need for something better and how would you do it?

I literally have sat down and I came up with a list of twenty things that are hot businesses. I did that in an afternoon just sitting down. Whether or not I pursue those, that's another story.

People think 'Oh, it's so competitive in this world.' Yeah, it's highly competitive in what already exists. Don't go out and try to do the same thing, try to find a new way to do it.

If you really sit down and do that, not only will you have a business, but you'll actually be revelled by the media for doing something that's new and unique. And if we had time, I would talk about some of those things that we're doing that would totally change the paradigm of how people are looking at our business.

**Tracey:** Just to finish up, where to from here? Have you got any last words of wisdom that you haven't yet shared that you want to share?

**Paul:** I think that there is a cycle in everyone's life of what we're going to do. I think when you first start out you go to school and you learn. I don't think you learn much. I think you learn how to think, that's the key thing. For anyone who's still in school, stay in school and do your homework because of what it's teaching you. I studied, whatever, geography. I can't tell you which way is up, my geography is horrible. I won't remember all the algebra, all the things that I learned, all the calculus and geometry, but it taught me how to think systematically. When I actually do have to write something or I have to think mathematically or geographically, I can approach it from a different angle. So first of all, realise that school is very valuable to teach you how to think.

Second thing is when you get out of school, get a job that will teach you as much as you can. Find a mentor. Go work for a company that will teach you as much as you can. Do not try to focus on being rich, focus on trying to learn what it is you want to get into.

Again, maybe even before you go to college, what are you passionate about? What do you really want to do? If you're lucky enough to know what it is, great. If not, don't beat yourself up. Go to college. You're going to come out, you're going to do something totally different than what you studied, it's totally fine. If it taught you how to think, that's cool.

Go work and do what you love to do. Learn from someone who can teach you as much as you can. Then, when you have enough experience and when you truly understand all the things that you need to understand about running a business, if you can't get that at your work experience, take classes. There's lots of online courses you can do at night if you're working during the day.

When you're ready, you can start your business. Understand that your first business, it might be a booming success or it might just be a learning experience, but never give up, keep going, Try more businesses, try again, try again. I'm on my third business now. All of them have succeeded. I have been fortunate, but each one becomes much more successful.

Now for me, I'm fortunate enough that I'm financially stable so when I choose to sell my business, if I want to sell my business, I can. You do have to have an exit plan. If you're starting your business always understand your exit plan. This will not be for life. If you don't have an exit plan, you're not thinking ahead about how you can put away money for yourself, how you can prepare for your older age—because it's going to come.

We all get old, so you have to think about what do I need to think about today for when I retire? Then that brings you to the stage where maybe I'm at, which is at some point I'm going to shift what I'm doing, because financially I have enough money. A lot of people want to keep going and making more money. I think personally, I just want to make as much as I need, not more than that, because there's a lot more to life than working. If you're excited about things and passionate about things, there's a million things that you can do in this life that are not about making money.

That's kind of where I'm going. How do I give back to the community? How can I help out? How can I really make a difference globally on environmental and on a human basis? How can I improve people's lives? So where I'm going is towards altruism.

I can really add value. I'm not looking to make money in those ventures. If we do, great, but never have I been looking to make money from some of it, even more so as I don't need the money. I can move away from the money side and do more for what really needs help, where I can really add value. Then at some point, you can look back and look at all that you've planted and all that's been harvested and all that you've created as a legacy.

I don't think it's about ego when you look at legacy. It's about how we really made a difference, how can we be of service in life to others, to the earth. We're going to go back into it, we're going to die and do we want to look back and say 'I was just someone who sat on the couch and watched TV and that was my great addition to life' or 'I pushed numbers in a company.' Do you want to look back and say 'You know, in my life, let me tell you about all the things I did to help people, to help the environment, to help make an improvement overall.' That feels really good internally. It's an exciting journey when you go that way, because it's for a bigger purpose.

## *After the interview* . . .

To be honest, Paul really surprised me. I didn't know a lot about him prior to the interview and so I had no expectation as to what it would be like. After I left the interview, I took time to reflect upon what Paul had said and how I could implement it in my life.

Paul was normal. By that I mean, he wasn't flashy. Just an everyday man. Yet, when he spoke, he struck a chord with me. He's not in it for the money. Even after the interview, we chatted and he said, 'How many boats can you waterski after anyway?' meaning it's not about the 'things.' This was clearly obvious as we left Paul's home to get coffee and do the interview. Paul took the time to say goodbye to his wife and his son who were both at home. No yelling 'See ya' at the door, it was a face-to-face goodbye. That impacted me.

The learning, that I want to share the most, came after the interview. This is what Paul talked to me about.

**Paul:** I have a house on the hill with a view for a reason, because I think big. I mean that contributes to my thinking not in a little way, but in a big way. Kings and queens used to have their castles up on the hill for a reason. They had this big grand view of the world and they're people, just like you and me. Now what if we all could be living up on a hill with a big view, wouldn't we have a bigger vision? So that's the idea, is getting people to get the bigger vision, but not to be that greedy king or queen, but to say, okay, we're all in the community here and then knowing when to say enough is enough.

Where are you working on your vision for life? Take Paul's advice. Get out, go away, dream big. You don't have to live on a hill, but you can certainly go sit at the top of one for a while and dream and plan. People thought I was crazy, flying to the USA and travelling around, yet it made me think big. Paul made me understand why.

Another thing Paul talked about after the interview was about doing business in the future. It was so valuable that I want to share it with you.

**Paul:** I think to me it's about this new realm of entrepreneur who is conscious about more than just reaping, or raping the earth, taking from people, sapping people's energy. It's just if you can get the word out, 'Hey, you can be much more than that,' I think that there is going to be quite a movement.

I have a sixteen-year-old stepson and it's really hard right now, with all the things that they have to study and the competitive nature of things. What I keep trying to tell him is 'Are you just going to be another cog or are you going to go out in the world?'

I see this new generation who's so disenchanted with everything that's been going on with the economy. I mean this recession happened for a reason. All this stuff is happening, all the ways that we used to do things, they don't work anymore. We have to change entirely the way that we're approaching life, our business, our border relations. We have to all work together and we have to think about global warming, the environment and all these things, and it's not about capitalism. All the big capitalists are getting knocked down to their knees for a reason. The old way isn't going to work anymore.

We can't have any more entrepreneurs with too much money. I think if you can get the word out that the new entrepreneur is the entrepreneur who's building things that make a difference. They are also not being greedy about it, they're giving back and they're understanding where they need to give back and where their talents can add even more value once they're at a stable area. I don't want to make money just to have money. I want to make money to buy clarity. If I can go spend a week in the islands, I can do some amazing thinking. I can get some space versus being stuck in a cubicle.

Thanks Paul for your wisdom and for sharing with us so that we can all be so much more in our lives and in the world.

For more information about Paul, check out:

www.fetchpetcare.com

*Introducing...*

# Amy Bates-Stumpf

You can tell how successful people are by what they can handle. In the days leading up to my interview with Amy she was running her entire business from her Blackberry as her family had been evacuated from their LA home due to major fires in the area.

The morning we sat down to chat at the new location of my hotel, the school had just reopened and she had to attend a PTA meeting. Yet, her business was still running and she still sat with me.

After our meeting she was off to deliver food to the fire fighters because she feels it is important to be a part of your community. My Mum says if you need a job done, ask a busy person. This is Amy.

I had an amazing chat with Amy. She was so honest about business and her own personality traits and how they help or hinder her in business. I discovered things to help me, I hope you do too.

## *Interview with Amy Bates-Stumpf...*

**Tracey:** Tell us a little about your story. How you ended up in your business, what the initial idea was for it?

**Amy:** The initial idea wasn't even mine, so I have to give credit where credit's due. A good friend of mine, with kids in the same grades as mine, lives less than half a mile away. I met her through the elementary school. When I first got to know her, I had no idea what she did, what her background was, what this business was. It was really just kind of a fluke. She had called me from her business line and the caller ID said 'The Gift List'. The next time I saw her, I asked her what it was. She goes, 'Oh, it's this little thing and I'm not really sure I'm going to keep it going. It was an idea I had, but I don't really want to keep the business running, I want to get rid of it.' And that was that.

My situation at the time was that we had just moved to this new house and it was a huge expense. I had a two-year-old, a four-year-old and a five-year-old and my oldest one was in private school. That's why we had moved, because we wanted to be in a school district where we could send all our kids to the best schools and keep them in the neighbourhood. So we moved to this neighbourhood that we can't afford.

At the time I had a consulting business where I did mostly business communications and a lot of my clients, my big ticket clients, were government agencies.

Right after we moved, the Calgary state budget crisis happened and everything all of a sudden crashed and all state contracts were on hold. You could work against them and take an IOU, but there was no guarantee that you would ever get paid. All outsourcing was then—no more outsourcing.

So I knew even if I worked through some of these budgeted contracts that I had already signed, I knew that that was the end. Maybe not forever and it certainly wasn't forever, but we were not in a financial position for me to just all of a sudden not be working.

I was kind of at the point with the consulting where I just felt that I couldn't write another sentence. I had written for twenty years. I mean you could fill a football field with the paper of what I had written. That was what I did, that was my job. I could take concepts and ideas and condense them into whatever you needed. Do you need a press-release? Do you need a speech? Do you need a booklet? What is it that you need? That was what I did.

Often times I would run with large meetings and we would solicit public information and I could condense it down for different audiences. I really felt that with the small kids and the lack of sleep, the energy and focus that it takes to write coherently was something that I was just feeling I couldn't do anymore. I just didn't have that desire and I was losing a lot of motivation. So it just seemed like 'everything is falling apart' and we need to figure out what we were doing. I was at a point where I had nothing.

So I had asked my friend about this business. Never thought about it and it wasn't until probably a month later that she came back to me and said, 'I'm really thinking about getting rid of this business, do you want to talk about it?' She had come up with the idea from working at large PR firms, where she dealt mostly with consumer products. The challenge of dealing with seasonal and gift guides is they're very lateral, not vertical. Where let's say the health products, you could buy a beat list of health editors and it's a very vertical list, it's all health editors cutting through all sources of media. But gift guides are really different.

You can have a health product that might be appealing to all different kinds of editors and media of all different types because it could have a different hook or just maybe the hook is that it's like a gift under fifty dollars or something—it doesn't matter what it is. Putting those lists together was a huge challenge for these companies and she decided that she would create a little packed, condensed list for quality gift guides.

I think she really liked doing it, she liked creating the product. She liked talking to the editors and doing the interview and compiling it.

But then when it came to actually selling it and she realised that she wasn't doing PR and she wasn't talking to the media, she was actually running a small business where she could be selling widgets of any kind and it didn't matter, because now she's running a small business and she's kind of like, 'Hmm, this isn't what I do and I don't really have an interest in this. I like PR. I want to write and I want to talk to the media, but now I've created this situation where I'm now not doing that. I'm running a business and I don't want to do that'.

So I bought the idea from her for what seemed like a huge amount of money, due to the fact that we had no money. We had put everything into the house and so from a combination of borrowing from my parents and taking out a home equity line, I purchased the idea from her and started running the small business portion of the idea.

The idea was there and she'd done it for a couple of years. There was a really positive response—people loved the idea. She had a small group of sort of insider clients and she kind of worked with them and didn't have a plan for going outside of that. That was in 2003.

Now it's a very different business. I sort of expanded the Gift List idea to look at more than just the December holidays. We do spring, so we're doing Mother's Day, Father's Day, graduation and weddings and other stuff that happens in spring. The December holidays are the December holidays, we don't need to expand, they're big enough.

We've really taken it from just the idea and grew it and I liked the small business part of it. That was the thing that to me I kind of felt like, 'God, I could be selling anything.' I was just like, 'Put work in front of me and I'll do it.' It didn't really matter what it was, because it wasn't what I was doing before.

I had enough experience in the world of communications that I knew the lingo and I knew the process and I understood media. I've written speeches and dealt with press releases and I understand how communication works and where the sources of information are and where they need to go and how that needs to be. I really just needed to educate myself on the specifics of consumer products and what about them is special and unique. How to transfer that information to my clients in a way that makes them successful in using the information that I'm providing to them.

But it's been a challenge. I like the small business part of it and I think in many ways I'm looked at as a PR expert on consumer products, and holidays specifically, but I think there's so many people that are probably much more informed than I am, who have much more experience in doing that specifically. I feel so much more connected to the entrepreneur and I look at my product as, well I don't know, I mean I don't want to say this too much, but I have a lot of big corporate clients and I really look at it as a way to level the playing field because I know what it's like to be on the small end. There are entrepreneurs that are literally at their kitchen table running their business and they're using the exact same information to pitch their product that a big name brand, multinational company hiring a huge PR firm is using—the same information.

Do they have the same resources behind it? You know, maybe not, but the media doesn't always know that, especially in the age of technology. I really feel there's sort of like a grass roots to me. I feel like this is like little people using the exact same information. They follow the rules. They are creative and can push their ideas out to the media using that tool, they can get as much exposure as a big name company that everyone would know, a household brand name. So I like that. I think that's sort of the cool thing about it that's appealing to me and that kind of keeps me going.

There's a lot of drudgery in work, a lot of tediousness about running your own business, so you have to have something. At the end of the day I spent an hour talking to this guy who still has a full time job, and he has this idea and then I'll talk to him again a year later and he had a lot of success and is so grateful and I'm like, 'Oh, that's the best, he quit his job.' I'm like, 'That's awesome.'

**Tracey:** So how would a client go about using The Gift List or your services? What sort of process do they go through?

**Amy:** It's all online. To backtrack just for a second, when I bought the concept and the business from my friend, the way she gathered the data was initially she did the phone calls herself and then soon realised that that was just not possible. It was all done on paper.

The data collector would make the interview call, write it out onto a piece of paper and then every week she would get Fedexed the papers that she would give to a typist who would type them into a database.  Proofing was a huge problem because it was handwritten to typing. You had no real idea, so mistakes went through and it went out on a CD, so when you caught a mistake you had no way of communicating it.  The FedEx and the paper thing, I don't want to say she was a technophobe, but that wasn't her thing.

I love technology. I'm a gadget freak and I love the internet and online and I want to get rid of all paper in my office entirely.  That was my next big investment the year after I bought the business. I did it her way the first year, because I think that you can't change something until you really understand—maybe there's some logic behind what it was. There were certain ideas that I had that worked but the big thing that I changed is we went to a virtual office and we put the list online.

That made a huge difference because I didn't have to go some place. I didn't have to hire, everyone didn't have to be in LA and I didn't have to have an office and I could be at home. That made everything different.

I have little kids and I could work the hours that I needed to work and I could still be connected 24/7 with all of my staff. We could do iChat and do video, we did GoToMeeting, but now we do Yammer and other things where we're just constantly in communication with each other.

We all work off the same server so we're technologically linked, communication-wise we're linked and we all work as a team. If I'm not sitting at my desk and someone types a question into Yammer I've got fifteen other people that can probably answer it and everyone can communicate that way. We can get tips and hints to each other, problems, troubleshooting. So bringing everything to the internet and communicating through the internet was huge. So that got translated to the customer.

How someone would actually come to me and use the list is they would log on and what they're actually purchasing is access to view the data. They're not buying the data, I own the data, the data's always under my control.

That's important to me because I'm selling personal information about other people and I have to have legal control of that. If an editor calls me and says, 'I'm so inundated, I can't have another email', they're like 'I cannot take anymore', I'm like, 'You're off the list' and I can do it instantly. If I send that information out on CD or excel files or whatever, I can blast out that email but there is no guarantee that even a third of those people will even get the email and probably one percent of those people will actually stop pitching to that editor. The only way that I can have control is to remove them from the eyes of my customers.

Sometimes what we do is we leave their name in there, but we take out the contact information. I have an alert system where when they bring up that person it'll be in big, bold letters at the top 'This editor has plenty of information. Do not pitch for holiday anymore.' Or, 'This editor is complaining that they're getting pitches that are not in alignment with the stuff that they're interested in. Please review.' We can communicate to the customers on an instant basis anything that comes back to us from the editors.

That said, the editors don't contact me that often. We have really good researching and I think my customers buy the list because they really want to do something other than an email blast. They wouldn't buy my information if they didn't want to use it. They really want to know the specifics because they want to utilize the media.

I mean maybe out of fourteen hundred records in the database, maybe three editors might call to say, 'I'm getting some wonky stuff, can we go over what's in my profile and maybe make some adjustments?'

Staff changes faster than the speed of light these days. At the end of 2008, there was a huge media staff shake up, so that list was just in flux for about two months. We were making daily changes.

That is why I think that the internet makes me a more responsive vendor to my customers and it gives my customers so much more value when they do not have to be manually making updates, because the updates are happening all the time.

So they can log in, they put in their account information, just like you would basically buy a book from Amazon, there's really no difference in the shopping cart. They create a username and password and once they have that then they can go log in to whichever database that they've bought and within that database there are standard search mechanisms that will help them. They can do a keyword search for food, beauty, fashion, they can search by women's magazines, men's newspapers, they can search by North Carolina. They may have a local pitch, for example, the economy is a big hook these days. If you are doing all onshore production then the local areas want to know about that. Those are jobs that have stayed home, those are resources that are being purchased here stateside.

Let's say your production is in North Carolina. Well there's a lot of newspapers and regional magazines that cover that area and you can put them in, so you can search by that. There's a multitude of ways.

Then create pitching lists, they can export them to mail merge labels if they want to send out samples, if they want to send out a hard copy cover letter. Most people do it electronically, but they can still mail merge bits of information to personalise a kind of a standard pitch. They can get that in there.

We try to think of ways that we can format the data for them in a way that will help them use the economy of scale without making it seem boilerplate. We're in touch with them about things that they want. Maybe break out the fields a little bit so that they can use them and different things.

You know, it kind of depends, but essentially we're really about the interview. We're on the phone doing data collection the old-fashioned way and that's my staff, 90 percent of the people that work for me are on the phone interviewing the media and everyone else is just back office.

**Tracey:** So if you're interviewing the media, obviously they're happy with the end result as well, because they're getting better pitched stories to them.

**Amy:**  That's the idea, that my customers would be favoured—at least not blacklisted.  I think there's a real lazy way technology has been great, in that you can reach thousands of people for very few dollars. Whereas when I pitched the media fifteen years ago, twenty years ago, everything was hard copy.  The cost of the press kit alone, the colour printing, the assembling of it—you didn't just ship those things out willy-nilly—that was like a ten dollar packet, plus shipping. It was very different.

Now you can write a little email and it's essentially free, but it kind of comes back to bite you.  If you're just blasting out two thousand people, you're going to get a percentage of those people that you might need later on, but they don't want to ever hear from you again.  The editors are so sick of being inundated with inappropriate boilerplate pitches. It's very simple to just block an address and then you never can get through to them again. You might not even know either. You might be communicating to them and it's just being set aside. You can block an email address very easily.  They can block your whole domain.

So technology is great but you have to know how to use it in a way that, I mean really it's about respect I think, using it in a responsible way and a smart way. You're in business, you should be thinking about yourself and how it affects you.

Essentially that's what they're doing, they're looking at the data. That data that we're collecting is, we're asking now for the holiday list for example. 'Are you doing a holiday gift bag?' Yes, okay, so then there's a whole other line of questions. The flow chart of questions gets pretty branched up. They're doing a holiday gift bag. Does it have a title, because that's a great thing to put in the pitch, 'I have the perfect gift for your 'Pamper Mums this Christmas', or your 'Great gadgets under $100'.  If it has a title and you can put that in your pitch, then that immediately says to the editor, 'Hey, they've done their homework' and they love you. What are you looking for? Do you have a price point? All the different things that you would want to know.

One year a few years ago, *Parade Magazine* holiday gift guide was themed polka dots. It didn't matter what it was, it could be chair, it could be shoes, it could be a laptop case—polka dots. So if you've got that information, if your product's not polka-dotted, you can forget about it. If your product is polka-dotted you can get a sample in the mail the next day and hound them. You don't stalk them, but you can be on top of it.

You don't want to do anything that might cause alarm. That's something that is so precious to the publicist who's busy and overworked and has a lot to do.

Then sometimes they don't have that kind of information. Maybe they're not doing a holiday gift guide, but they're going to do gift suggestions. Or maybe it's in the food department or the features department of a newspaper and they're doing holiday entertaining and it's not gifts. But I have a lot of food customers, quite a few food customers, because people eat around Mother's day, Father's day, graduation, weddings, proms and holidays. So food is big.

It's not always a gift. Sometimes it's a gift, and gift baskets do well, but they want to be able to develop a recipe. They'll pitch the recipe, table top stuff, sometimes buying it as a gift, but it's a way to decorate. You can pitch a whole story on that, but your dishes or knick-knacks or whatever are being incorporated.

We look at not just the gift guides, but any kind of holiday theme. If they cover consumer products every month, they're going to still cover them in December, whether it's holiday related or not, so we will include them as well. We generally won't give them a deadline, because we consider them evergreens and we don't want people rushing to maybe prioritise them over something that has a real deadline, so that's coded in the list. Then they can put them on the backburner and pitch them at some other time or for December, it doesn't matter. So anything that's consumer product related we want to know. We want to know the types, fashion, not fashion, whatever, beauty but not hair care, who knows?

Then we ask them how they want to get their things delivered and do you accept on my links, emails, emails with no attachment, plain text only? Long, long options that are all based on the interview questions, but on our list they're checkboxes that get translated.

We went to the checkboxes for proofing reasons and to make it a little bit more standardised for the reader, for the customer. Because they're reading a lot of information and if every description has a different voice, you can't get through it as quickly. We have a lot of checkboxes as well as getting images to them because you can't send twenty by ten megabyte images, you will crash their system and you need a way to find out how they want it.

Some people don't want images, sometimes they're fine with huge images and love huge images, they've got tons of email space. So we asked them all about that and it's just sort of to give our customers that little leg up, kind of hedge their bet against all the competition to at least get the information to them in a way that's not going to anger the recipient and will in fact impress them.

Anything else that we can add in there, we do. Maternity leave, just sort of a special quote that really conveys the personality of the editor who wants to make each record as standardised in the sort of fact stuff, but then really personal in the individual stuff. So it's a good balance and we try to get as close to the mark as we can on fifteen hundred records in six months and then we start all over again.

We're working around the clock, because literally the last post that goes up for the holidays, the very next week is the first post for spring, because they're exactly six months apart. The only hiatus we take is a little bit in the summer between the magazine and getting through the broadcast and then again around in April. But it's constant and the editors know us now, they learn to sort of expect the call. We get a lot of good feedback from them and they'll take our call now because they know it's not a pitch and it's a quick interview that we know how to get what we need. They can vent out everything they need and we take it all down.

So that's the system and all of that is just typed into a database and my customers log in with their username and password and look at it and they can have everyone in their office looking at it at the same time, everyone can be creating their own pitching list.

They have unlimited amount of access to create as many customised lists as they want, so everyone can work together. There's internal subscriber notes where they can communicate about a particular record or, 'I contacted this person, they said XYZ, I'm going to send a sample.' Everyone in the staff will (just their staff that have their log in) will see that note, so they can communicate internally. All that stuff came from customer feedback, from asking them, 'How do you use it? What would be good to add?' It's not that difficult.

With a good programmer, you can really deliver on things that seem like specialised requests. I have an excellent programmer. I love my programming team, they are awesome. I can say, 'Someone said they'd like to do the thing where the gig does that,' and he's like, 'Oh, okay.' And then like the next day I can see it in beta, I mean, amazing. They're in Connecticut.

And that's how I am, everyone is all over the country. I have data collectors in New Jersey and Michigan and Tennessee, because the virtual office has given me the opportunity to pick the best people and not just the local people. It's great.

**Tracey:** How did you discover your passion? Like people are always asking me, 'How do I find my passion? How do I know when I just love it?' And listening to you, you just love it. So did you discover that, did you purposely go out to find it? Or did it just sort of crop up along the way?

**Amy:** I think I knew early on that I needed to work for myself and that is just the way I am. I've worked for Government agencies, so they're like the whole other end of the spectrum.

I think if you asked my parents, they'd say that at an early age I needed to be in an environment where—it isn't that I need to be the boss—but I need to be independent. I don't know, maybe I'm not a good team player, who knows? I do like to have the final say on some decisions, but I'm very open to advice and I'm not bashful about asking for help because I know that there are a lot of things that are not my expertise, like budgeting and business planning.

The budget is something that I look at, it could be written in another language. It means nothing to me. My personality is something that I don't ever look at the budget before I make a spending decision, so I do know that I need help and I have like three people dealing with my money because I can't, it's not my thing.

But I have someone doing accounts payable and someone doing accounts receivable and I have the third person who reconciles those things because I could not find a mistake if I was alone in a room for ten years. I couldn't figure it out because it's not my thing. I know that, because that's not my thing and because I won't want to be working 24/7 and make no money that I need to hire good people who know what they're doing and that I trust. I don't know why I need three people, but I just do it that way. They're not working full-time.

I like to hire independent contractors for everything and not just because I don't want to do payroll, it's really just because I want them to feel that they've got ownership in what they're producing for me, because I'm an entrepreneur and I want them to be an entrepreneur. I want them to be given a project and take ownership of that and feel like they're delivering me what they do for a living.

This is what they do and here they are delivering that, as opposed to like a punch in a time clock. I want them to feel that they own it and they do. They have access to the media, they have access to customers who have questions about that. And I monitor, obviously, I see all the emails that come through just to make sure that information is correct and my company is being presented how I want it to, but I really want them to feel that they've got a lot of freedom from me and that they have a lot of accountability. So that's why I like the independent contractors.

**Tracey:** How many people would be able to get on the phone and speak to an editor of a magazine?

**Amy:** Not many. No, I now hire freelance journalists and I think the marriage is great. I don't want someone working forty hours a week making phone calls, because by the end of the eight-hour day, the enthusiasm is not there. No one can smile and dial for eight hours a day, five days a week and I don't want that.

We're really strict about all the phone calls to the editors. They have to be made between nine thirty and eleven thirty in the morning and they have to work East Coast to West Coast if they want to work more than two hours a day. Which most of them do, obviously.

That's really important to me. I want the editors to have that first cup of coffee and I don't think it's fair to call them in the afternoon because a lot of them are on deadline and they're busy and no one really wants to be bothered in the afternoon. By the time three o'clock hits, everyone is like 'Oh my God, I can't believe I've gotten nothing done.' I mean that feeling is universal and the last thing you need is a call that's not revenue-generated, it's not a pitch that's going to help you finish that story. It's certainly not helping you get to deadline any quicker.

We're asking a huge favour of them, their time is so precious, and we need like fifteen to twenty minutes of it, so this is a big thing. I really want to catch them in the best mood and at the most convenient time. They work East Coast to West Coast and then that gives them as much time as they need to pursue their freelance writing. I'm sure they switch hats, they might do a few data collection calls and then 'Oh, you're working on that story?'

I do lose people every once in a while. I had a really great data collector that got hired by Lucky, which was great for her but bad for me. Although I have an inside line now.

They like it because it not only gives them flexible hours working from home in their jammies, but they can do all the things that people say you do when you work from home. I don't work in my jammies, but it's like that's sort of the dream of the home business, that for some reason you don't have to get dressed. But work that actually helps them in the other thing that they do, that I would assume is probably more valuable, that is their passion.

Doing interviews on the phone isn't what they see themselves doing forever, they're journalists. So it's a good marriage. It's great for me because I only pay them for the hours that they need to work to finish the project and they can pick those hours within pretty loose guidelines, we've got a big country, there's a three-hour time difference, they can really work hours that they need and they can start super early in the morning if they want to and still have their day.

The only downside is if they get a gig that is going to be taking up a lot of their time or cause them to be travelling or just not be available during the times that I want them to be calling editors, then they have to leave. I've got to replace people immediately. This is a deadline sensitive product, we cannot take our time to hire someone else, so I am always on the lookout for people waiting in the wings that we may need to kick into gear like immediately. That stresses me out. That's a big stress for me that I live in fear of losing a data collector in the middle of peak season, that's a big thing.

**Tracey:** So what do you think has been the greatest skill you've had to develop through the years for your business?

**Amy:** Time management, hands down number one, is almost the only skill I needed. The only skill. I can deal with people naturally, that's not a problem and I feel, by nature, I'm generous with my time. People call me asking questions. I don't have an issue with helping, even when it doesn't directly relate to the product. I like people, I enjoy it. Being in a customer-based business has been great for me personality-wise.

I get really behind with emails and getting in touch with people and that's really not out of lack of desire to get back to them. It's that I will spend way too much time. I'm not efficient with my communication. I need to ask for help, but I have a hard time doing that.

Dealing with the customers is kind of like the last vestige of letting other people in. Help with the bookkeeping, oh, no problem, bring it on. Helping with the graphic design, not my thing. Programming, go for it. Talking to my customers, hmm, let's think about that for a minute.

But I can't as the customers grow. When I had one hundred customers, no problem. Three hundred customers, I'm up until two in the morning. As it grows and grows, I have three hundred emails in my inbox right now.

Obviously, due to the fire and the evacuation I'm working off my Blackberry. It's tough and I will catch up, but during peak season I can easily have one hundred unopened emails a day and I know that this is the last year that I'm going to be able to do this by myself, I know it. I've got to start training someone to get them on board, because it's just not good for me, it's not good for the business and the last thing I want to do is upset my customers because I can't get back to them. That is the next thing that I know I have to do.

My biggest reward was being at home, having three children grow up. I bought the business when my youngest was two, he's now almost nine. My oldest was five and he's now thirteen. Sarah was four, she's now eleven, huge difference.

When my youngest actually started school full-time, two years ago and he was in school from eight to two and I had all that time alone for the first time since I could remember, it was unreal. It was so quiet—it was just me and the dogs in the house. I quickly learned to fill that time and in a very short period of time, it went from this long day to 'They're home already?'

But that changed everything for me, because I no longer had to stay up until two in the morning and fall asleep at my keyboard, which was not good, not good for anyone. I mean that was just bad, but that was the only way. I could have hired a nanny and had day care and I just didn't do that. I was 'I'm working at home and the kids would be home.' Isn't that the whole idea?

Even the summer I spent a good deal of the time sitting at my computer with a remote control helicopter circling my head and people would come into the office, 'How are you working?' I know no other way, that is what I would say. 'I don't know, how do other people work?' This is how I do it, dogs barking, kids running around, fixing snacks every hour—when they're home, they're home.

But I think that structuring your time is important when you live and play and work in the same four walls. I have a separate office with its own bathroom and a hallway and it's very separate from the rest of my home, but it's not a mile away. I can walk there in two seconds.

It's not like I can't get into it or someone locks me out. I mean I can always get there and I could take refuge there if I wanted as well and just work around the clock and never answer my phone or make a bed or feed my kids. And I think you would end up really depressed. I think you would end up really depressed and really unhealthy because you'd eat jelly beans all day.

Do you know what I mean? It's not just the working, it's everything. You'd stop exercising and you'd stop cooking and you'd stop socialising and going out to lunch with a friend or happy hour with your husband or something. You could just be in there all the time, because the work is never-ending and it always seems like it's important. If you kind of didn't want to do all that other stuff, it can become sort of like your ace in the hole or just like the all purpose excuse and you'd end up really sad. It's like no one looks back on their life and says, 'God, I wish that I had locked myself in the office for ten years and never left.' I mean, no one says that. No one says, 'God, I spent way too much time with my kids' or 'I wish I'd just eaten TV dinners every night because all that organic food was just too hard.' I mean no one says that they wish that they'd never had a family dinner, people don't do that.

I can waste time like it's nobody's business. I can. I hate to admit that. It's not that I'm being lazy, I'm being actually really active, but I'm doing stuff that is unnecessary. I can get online and go far, deep in something that has nothing to do with anything except just some remote interest of mine. If that's your personality, maybe some people aren't like that, but working at home, you're alone and you can get lost in that alone, your own head space. You don't have co-workers constantly asking you a question that would get you back on track.

**Tracey:** Has there ever been a time when you doubted yourself and what you could achieve?

**Amy:** Oh, every day. It's not really putting the cart before the horse, it's more I tend to jump into things like the business.

I didn't really know that much about it. I just knew that it sounded like something that I wanted and once I'd decided that I wanted it, I had to have it. I become very focused on that. I have made business decisions, with this business, I expanded too quickly and I've had to close down aspects of the business after investing upwards to maybe like one hundred thousand dollars into something. I just decided, you know what, I'm just throwing good money after bad and I did not do my homework, I jumped in too quickly, I don't like it, I find that I avoid it. And guess what? Bye-bye.

It's kind of hard to do that because there's that cognitive dissonance, it's sort of like standing in a really long line and then you get to the point like, 'Do I really want what's at the end of that line? But I've invested so much damn time in this line I'm not leaving, I'm getting to the head of that line if it's the last thing I do.' I think everyone has that feeling of like, 'Well I've put in so much time, energy, money, frustration, and I'm going to stick this thing out.'

Someone has to kind of say to me 'What the hell are you doing?' It took a while. A couple of people were saying to me, 'Well, why are you doing that?' 'I don't know, because I made the decision to do it.' That's really stupid. You almost have to say it out loud, because they're like, 'Well, why would you divert money into something that isn't as profitable? Why would you divert money into B when A is more profitable and put time into B when A needs more.' I'm thinking 'Yeah, that makes sense, why didn't I think of that.' But you knew it, but you couldn't let go.

It's not even really admitting failure, because who am I admitting it to? I mean yourself, I guess and maybe that's the hardest person to admit it to, but it isn't really for me. I was okay with it being like, 'You know what, I screwed up. I made a decision.' Like, you know, whatever.

Then once you do that, for me at least, the pain of the money having been spent doesn't last that long. It was just like the monkey off my back, 'Oh my God, I'm done with that. I'm done with the employee I don't like whom I felt was taking advantage of me. I'm done with the product that I didn't really understand as well as I thought I did. And I just am so glad to be done with it.' It felt so good and I'm hoping that I will take that lesson with me.

I do find that it's like I jump into things, maybe before I really know, because I've always been the kind of person. I'll just make it work. I always land on my feet and it'll be okay because I kind of have the mentality that like hard work figures everything out. But it isn't really the case. That's not true because hard work doesn't always make things work. I have always felt like you can just pile work in front of me and I'll just do it. I'm a worker bee in a lot of respects. Like it doesn't matter what I'm doing, I can just get it done because I am focused and I can just do it, it doesn't matter what it is.

But that doesn't make you money, it just makes you tired. It makes you productive, but it doesn't really make you productive in the things that are going to make money for you or make you happy—it just really makes you productive. I was a very productive person my whole life, but not everything that I produced needed to be produced. So it's looking at that and it's tough, because you're fighting against your personality. There's certain things about my personality that make me so suited for running my own business and really making it hugely successful and there are parts of my personality, like this, that make me think, 'What the hell am I doing?' Like I might like what I'm doing, but I could be making a lot more money if I just wasn't the way I am. You kind of have to say that, you have to say, 'I am the only one to blame. It's just me.'

**Tracey:** So how did you build belief in yourself to keep going and to keep succeeding? Do you have any daily disciplines?

**Amy:** No, I think I was just born with that misconception. That's the thing, like I feel that I can just do anything. That feeling of, 'Well whatever it is I will get it done through figuring it out and putting time in it, just through hard work. Whatever it is I will get it done and I will do it the way I want to do it.' It's just a personality thing. It's like more of just the tenacity of, 'Well, I think I can do it, I don't care if you don't.'

**Tracey:** Have you had anyone ever doubt you, said, 'Oh, I don't think you can do that?'

**Amy:** Not to my face. I'm sure a boss, sure, definitely, who hasn't? But no one's actually said it to me in a serious way, not with business, not with something like this, no.

In fact I think people tend to say things to me that even I don't believe. Like the woman that I bought the business from. Every time we were in a situation, and it happens to maybe come up that I took over her business, she's always like 'Oh, she just skyrocketed this thing and believes she can do anything.' I'm thinking, no. I feel it was her idea, I still feel like I get all the credit of it. All I did was work really hard. I just got more customers and expanded it in different ways and took advantage of technology. Really, I can't take credit for the internet, I just use it. I feel like, 'It was your idea, it was you that did it.' To me it's all just hard work. This is my new project and I have to make it work. It has to make money or we can't stay in our house, we'd have to move.

**Tracey:** You were talking earlier, before we started the interview, about what would you put on your tombstone and those sorts of things. What are the things that you're learning in business that you really want your children to learn from watching you in business?

**Amy:** I think it's back to like I answered the question earlier, as being time management, but I think it's a priority.

For many years I was not a priority to myself at all. I came last and I think mums do that, but I really was last on the list. I mean there were years when I didn't even make the list. I'm not a martyr type, I was just so overwhelmed with having three kids in four and a half years and working and I never took time off work really. I mean brief times after the kids were born I would slow down on my consulting gigs just so that my hours would be light, but I took on a lot of volunteer work. I just took on way too much, because I wanted to do all those things but then in the end there just wasn't enough of me. There just wasn't enough of me to give what I needed to give to all these things that were going on, and so there was nothing left for me.

I think it's a cultural thing or gender-cultural, but it's easy to do that and I think I would really want to impart on my kids that if you do work for yourself, or even if you don't, that you need to figure out-time, even if it's just five minutes, where it's total silence and you just breathe.

You've got to figure out what do you enjoy doing and you need to do it. You don't want to be at the end of your life and look back and say, 'I really loved golfing, too bad I never golfed.' I mean it's like, why? What were you doing instead that was so critical? Really, what was so critical that you couldn't take three hours once a month to golf?

For me, it was exercise and all that. Even just getting my hair coloured. Nothing. I never did anything. Then it almost kind of hit me all at once. I am doing what I need to do or I will not make it, I will end up in the loony bin. I am like at the threshold of the loony bin, so it's now or never.

I think I never want my kids to be in that place. It's like you've got to figure out your time and when you figure out your time, you've got to make sure that you are not being neglected because you will be unhappy. If you're not happy, you will make everyone around you miserable. It's like that refrigerator magnet that says 'If Mum ain't happy, nobody's happy.' It's true, but it isn't just Mum, it's anyone.

No one wants to be around someone who feels neglected and who is mad about it. They don't want to be around those kind of people, so I think that there's a big gap between taking care of yourself and being totally self-indulgent to the point where it's obscene. There's a huge gap. You can take care of yourself and make your life full in the way that you pay attention to what your needs are—whether it's getting eight hours of sleep or exercising every day or taking time to just meditate or lunch every Friday afternoon with your best friend or whatever it is. They don't have to be big giant things, but they need to be on the list.

**Tracey:** So if someone came up to you and said, 'I just couldn't do what you've done', what would you say to them?

**Amy:** Oh, you absolutely could, I think so. Unless they were saying 'I really have a strong craving to own my own business. I have this idea and I would love it if I could do it, but I just don't think I could do it'. I'm like 'If you really want to do it, you can do it.' The thing is that you will not know until you try, so you need to do it.

**Tracey:** So where to from here? For you?

**Amy:** Right now I'm at sort of a crossroads with the business, because I'm now not looking at how to grow it. I still want to grow it, but when I first started there was no end in sight. I didn't think about that, it wasn't part of the plan. But now I think in ten years my little one will be off at college.

I travelled extensively in my twenties and it's hard to go to the places where I went and spent as little as I did with three kids. So I'd love to go back. I don't want to sleep in hostels, but I'd love to get back to some international travel and do something by myself and just my husband. I love being with my family, but there's got to be an upside to being in an empty nest. I haven't quite figured it out, but I keep thinking that it's going to be good and not worry about it.

I'm looking at the ten-year plan now in a way that I never did before. My little one is going to graduate in June 2019. That seems really far away, but I know that that goes 'like that'. I will have a teenager driving like on Tuesday. It all goes so fast, and I think in business, like in life, it goes fast.

You can plan for stuff, but it's not tragic if it doesn't go right. It's your perception and you enjoy your life and you enjoy what you're doing, but in business if the ten-year mark hits you and you are not prepared and you need to sell that business because you need the cash to do something with it, you're screwed. I mean obviously the day-to-day operations, but what I need to do is look at ten years from now, because it's really like ten years. I've never had a ten-year plan.

I've really only worked at like two and three-year plans. I never really even looked at the five-year plan because I was so brand new. Now I want to look at it, because I want to be able to sell my business. I look at it as the dream thing, because that's who I am. They might say that's totally unrealistic, but we'll get to that. When we get to it, we'll cross that bridge.

What I want to know is ideally if I could sell my business for this amount of money, how much revenue do I need to be generating to make it worth that amount? If I'm generating that amount of revenue, this is what I need to be doing. What is my budget going to look like? What do I need to actually do? And then look at year nine, eight, seven, six, five, four, three, two, now—make the decisions that I need to make, so that I can sell the business in ten years.

Maybe I'll decide not to sell, but I kind of think that at that point I'll have been doing it for ten years and knowing me I will be very ready to sell it. Although that seems really unfathomable, I can't imagine it, but I know that I will be at a life point that I'm going to need a clean break and something new and a new challenge. I really always need that.

**Tracey:** Do you have any last things that you want to add, any tips?

**Amy:** Don't be embarrassed that you work at home. Actually I think you've got to wave that flag high because I think it will change things for the better. It's almost like a social movement. Don't hide it. It isn't like you're out on the streets, certainly not a civil rights issue, but I think it's the more you stay closeted about it, the worse it gets.

It's like there's no way that it's going to become respected unless the people who are producing phenomenal quality work out of their homes are out there saying, 'I do this and I work from home and these are the reasons that I do it.' It's so much more about lifestyle and what you want to get out of your whole life, not just what you do sitting at your desk, because all of that factors in. If you are not happy and balanced in everything, you're not going to be a productive worker for yourself and if working at home makes you more balanced and happy, then you're going to produce more.

Renting an office, and going to that office and being miserable about it, doesn't make you better or more respected or more legitimate. It is perfectly legitimate to work at home. It doesn't matter, that office could be anywhere and you have to say it.

## *After the interview . . .*

What I learned from Amy was how to look at something that is working and make it even better. Everyday people want to get into business, but believe they need to invent something new or come up with a new idea.  Amy proves you don't have to. By using her skills and talents she was able to take a business to the next level and was the perfect person to do it.

A talent Amy has is creating a community through her business. It is no surprise, since she is so personally involved and committed to her local community.

Another trait that impressed me was her sense of thinking logically about things. Sometimes it is the littlest actions that create your success. For example, she and her team only call editors in the morning. Thinking about what works for the editors ensures her success and that of her clients.

Amy is a wife, a mother with young kids, a member of her community, a leader in her industry and definitely a woman in a home-based business who others can look to for inspiration.

Thank you Amy.

For more information about Amy, check out:

www.giftlistmedia.com

*Introducing . . .*

# Michael Epstein

Michael is one half of the partnership of eDimensional. How could I not include an interview with a guy who started a business with his friend from their college dorm rooms, with just $500? I am sure their story will redefine for you what is possible if you just get out there and do it.

Going into business with a friend can be a risky move. It seems like fun at the start, and everyone assumes that it will work out great. But as time passes, especially if a business is not succeeding, it can turn out to be a nightmare.

Michael and Nate are an example of how you can make it work. They are also a great example of doing whatever it takes to get the business to succeed, even if you have to eat noodles for a year.

## *Interview with Michael Epstein . . .*

**Tracey:** First of all, what I'd love to hear is your story. How you got started and how you've ended up here?

**Michael:** We started about ten years ago. Myself and my business partner, Nate, knew each other since we were kids. We were both from the Washington DC area. I was still going to school in the DC area, at University of Maryland, and working as the IT director for a management consulting firm. Nate was down here in Florida going to school.

We were always kind of bouncing ideas off each other about businesses that we would want to start to go into business for ourselves. While Nate was down here, he went to Universal Studios in Orlando and went on one of the 3-D rides—the movie rides where you put the glasses on and the movie pops out at you. He calls me after walking out of the ride and says, 'We should make people's video games do that.' I said, 'Okay, let's do that.'

So basically, the next day we decided to start a company and figure out how to do that, all while we were involved in school and other things.

So the first product that we kind of developed or came out with was these 3-D gaming glasses. The technology itself had previously been used in commercial applications like geomapping or molecular modelling, things of that nature, but we created software with the help of people that we had write this code for us. But it was our concept of software that would allow any regular video game off the shelf to be converted into this format, so that when viewed with our glasses, which we would purchase wholesale from some of these distributors, would appear in real 3-D—like 'come out at you' objects would be far off in the distance.

We started out basically purchasing these glasses in very small quantities at a time, wholesale. We got a friend of mine from college, who was learning how to write web code, to help build our website. We had a friend whose father was a partner in a law firm help us draft the incorporation documentation, and basically, just didn't know any better other than to move forward the only way we knew how. And we were running it out of our respective dorm rooms, far away from each other for a while.

Basically we spent the first year appealing to friends and family, trying to get the product out there, just to figure out how to sell it. We really had no idea. The interesting thing is Nate and I didn't really come from an extensive gaming background, we didn't start the company necessarily because gaming was our passion. It was more the entrepreneurial aspect that was our passion. We were really trying to figure out how to get it in front of the right target audience.

Eventually we started getting a sale here and a sale there through our internet website. One day towards the end of our first year, at the beginning of our Christmas season, we woke up and there were a bunch of orders on our website. Nate and I are calling each saying, 'This is great, we've made it.'

Meanwhile, we were nearing the end of our college experience and our parents were saying, 'We're cutting off the funds when you're done, so you need to figure out what you're going to do.' We were pretty much at a turning point where we had to decide, 'Are we going to pursue careers, a normal career with a big five firm or something like that, or really pursue this'? We were trying to calculate how many Ramen noodles we needed to live if we sold this many glasses.

We woke up this morning to a bunch of orders, a lot more than normal and we traced it back to a post on a flight simulation website, flightsim.com, which is the biggest flight simulation website.

Apparently somebody had bought our glasses and it made their flight simulation experience so much better. They posted about their experience and that kind of hit a nerve with that community, which is generally a bit of a more affluent and an older demographic that is looking for anything to make their flight simulation experiences as realistic as possible. Our glasses were a natural fit for that.

So once we traced it back we said, 'We've found a way to get sales', so we went full-force into promoting it in any flight simulation arena that we could find: website, partnering with companies to get it who wrote magazines and other print publications to get our product reviewed.

Then from there we kind of went to racing simulations. We figured that was the closest next step and eventually we started finding additional customers as well through using the same sort of marketing techniques, grass roots, getting reviews on different website and trading data advertisements for commission on sales, instead of fronting the money. Basically using the same methodology to get it in front of our target customer on no budget.

One thing worth noting is that we started with five hundred dollars and we never took out any loans. We never took out any additional debt. We were able to generate one million dollars of sales in our first full year, basically by using the same strategy and just replicating it over and over again—getting the product reviewed by different publications. That really reinforced it amongst their own readers and customers.

The 3-D glasses were really what got us started and still are a big part of our business. Since then we've rolled out a number of additional products like headphones and game controllers and tried to develop a retail presence as well, selling our products both directly through our website and also in retail stores in the US and in other countries.

After the first full Christmas season, we were generating enough sales so we could kind of be self-sufficient and not necessarily have to go out looking for additional jobs.

The interesting thing for me was that around this time I was still working for another company on almost a full-time basis, but this was around the time of the dot-com crash when a lot of the financing and money was drying up and the company I was working for was actually shutting down almost their entire business.

They laid off essentially the entire company. The timing couldn't have worked out better because to be honest, I don't know if I would have been able to make that step of saying, 'I am going to leave this company on my own to pursue this,' because it was going pretty well and I liked the job. When they said, 'All right, everybody's let go', Nate and I agreed that we have to get eDimensional going, we don't have a choice anymore because it's got to become our income. It was kind of a scary time—but an interesting and a challenging time. Right after that happened, Nate moved back to DC as he was finishing school, so that we could really pursue it full time.

The next step for the company was the basement of a townhouse in Alexandria, Virginia. Nate and I lived upstairs and worked out of this dark, just not nice townhouse. I remember when we were first moving in, we had a gaming chair product that we were selling and I don't even think we had a lot of furniture yet at that point. Nate slept in the gaming chair in the basement most of the time, for at least the first little while until we could get beds.

Basically we really just ran it on the smallest budget and the smallest amount of overhead that we could. It was not by choice, but I think that that's ultimately what's enabled us to remain successful through the years and continue to prosper right now, in a time that's particularly challenging.

From the start, we were always very disciplined about how we spent every dollar. We were always accountable for every dollar that we spent and never really got into any sort of extravagant working style or business style. We didn't know any different. Based on our office today, it's pretty obvious that we still haven't really splurged on things that aren't critical to growing the business.

We were in the townhouse, it was great because we were working 120 hour weeks, that was just the norm. We could basically pass out downstairs if we had to or we'd come up, take a nap for a few hours and then start again the next day. We used to say that FedEx would come to pick up at five or six o'clock at night and that was the half-time mark for us and we'd keep going.

We brought in some college and high school kids to start helping with the shipping and some of the basic stuff. We tried to get a couple of interns from local colleges who could use our business to earn college credit and we would help. Something that was kind of challenging as a side note to the intern process, is it sounds great because it's free labour, but it doesn't always work out that great. You have to have a really good, structured program and you really have to have the time to monitor their activities and spend time with them or else neither of you are really going to benefit.

The challenge was that as the business owner, and acting as the only employees that the company had, the interns required a lot of our time for instruction and monitoring of their activities. So even though it was free, you ended up spending a ton of your time overseeing everything that they did. Ultimately, as soon as they got kind of up to speed, their internship was over and then you'd have to start over again. So that was something that probably didn't work out as great as it could. But using high school and college kids for some of the basic tasks, like shipping and making the boxes and other things that we needed, that worked out really well. We could train them quickly. If they graduated high school and went off to college we could bring their friends in that were a year younger and it worked out pretty well.

We were in Virginia for a few years. This was when we were in our early twenties, about twenty-one and twenty-two years old. The very interesting thing about starting that young and the way we did it working out of this townhouse, the 'About us' page on our Web site certainly didn't show a close-up of the front door of our townhouse— instead we had a picture of an office building.

Nate and I would talk to business associates and partners about our wife and kids and these sorts of things and they said, 'Oh, we're going to come visit your office, we're going to be in the area.' Nate and I just happened to be out of town that weekend or something else. We went to great lengths to ensure that people didn't know exactly what our operation was for a long time.

When you're submitting a purchase order for one hundred thousand dollars and you're asking for thirty or forty-five day terms on it, I don't think they really want to know that they're giving the terms to a couple of twenty-one-year-old punks who are working out of the basement of their townhouse. That was something that we went through for a long time and actually it's probably been only very recently that we've really opened up. Now that we're thirty and people are starting young—I mean Facebook is run by twenty-four-year-old kids so it's really lost a lot of its stigma—but now it's become kind of more normal for us and, okay, we're a lot more open about it. We definitely went through that for a long time.

The next step for us was, we moved up to Northern Virginia. One, because it was near our family and two, because we thought it was the place to be. That's where AOL and that whole technology corridor was—in the Northern Virginia area. We thought we needed to be in that area. We're kind of this technology company and we thought it would benefit us to be surrounded by some of these other companies.

We learned pretty quickly that it was going to make no difference to us, we weren't going to be acquired by AOL or anything like that. The venture capital money that we thought might be something we were interested in was not really suited for us and not even really that readily available anymore by this time. So we decided to go where the weather was nicer and the taxes were lower and that was Florida, which we were familiar with because Nate had gone to school down here. I'd just visited a couple of times and we really like the area. We moved down here and set up an office.

We had two apartments next door to each other. One that we lived in and one that we worked in. That was the next step, from the basement to actually walking next door to the office. We just basically converted a regular two-bedroom apartment into an office.

Same sort of thing of having high school and college kids work for us doing the basic tasks. But it was basically Nate and I working out of there and outsourcing as much as we could in terms of programming, website maintenance, things like that, and just continuing to focus on sales and creating more efficiencies in the business, so that we could kind of be a little bit more scaleable when the time came for us to grow.

Operational efficiencies kind of went from handwriting every FedEx label and driving them over to FedEx at the end of the day—where they really hated us for that because we'd walk in at one minute to closing time with a car full of boxes, especially during the Christmas season, with all handwritten labels that they had to type in one at a time—to automating everything, printing everything out, having drivers come on a regular basis and things like that. We kind of reached that point by the time we got down here.

We were in that apartment for a couple of years. I had a girlfriend of a long time and she moved to Florida. She had still been in DC, which I think worked out particularly well because my work schedule was not conducive to that kind of relationship, so she was great to stick with it, I give her a lot of credit for it. It worked out well because we could focus on continuing to grow the business.

Once things started to stabilise for us (we'd been in business for six or seven years at this point and things were pretty stable) I decided to bring her down to Florida and that meant that Nate had to get kicked out of the apartment. We went looking for space and this time it was down the street. Nate actually ended up moving into the apartment that we were working out of previously and we found an office down the street, a mile away from us, that was a small office space, but it was actually located in a self-storage facility. So in addition to retail space they had storage space.

It was great for us because we had a lot of inventory, but it fluctuated a lot. We would order thousands of units at a time, sell them down to next to nothing over a period of time and then get thousands more. So we didn't really want to have a lot of office space that we were paying for, or warehouse space that we were paying for, when sometimes we had a lot, sometimes we had not a lot. This was great because we could get individual storage units. When we needed it, we rented it. When we didn't, we just gave it back. That worked out well for us and we were there for a couple of years and we continued to grow.

We added our flight simulation pilot shop, which is another part of our business, which instead of having all manufactured products that we make and distribute through stores, we retail other people's products in addition to ours. We ended up taking in a lot more products that we were keeping on a more consistent basis. We were at a point where we could finally find space that would suit us for this ongoing amount of inventory. So that's where we ended up—here about a year ago. We're on about twenty-five hundred square feet of mainly warehouse, with a little bit of office in the front. And so that's pretty much where we're at today.

**Tracey:** That's a great story. So some of the things you've spoken about that a lot of people have a lot of trouble with is a partnership, of working with someone else. What do you think has been the key for you and Nate to actually make it work?

**Michael:** It's definitely challenging. I mean Nate and I haven't been more than ten feet away from each other for ten years. It's fun and it's challenging.

I think one of the most important things you can do is separate your responsibilities so that you're not overlapping and people aren't stepping on toes. I know if I worked with somebody just like me I would have killed them in ten minutes, I mean there's no question that it would not have worked at all. I have a certain type of personality, a certain skill set and Nate has something that is very different from me.

Actually very early on, a business consultant came in and gave us this personality test, or skill set test, and we filled them out independently and when they showed us the results it was comical, the exact inverse results that Nate and I had. If I was 20 percent this way, he'd be 20 percent that way. If I was 80 percent this way, he'd be 80 percent that way.

I think part of it was, by nature, that was kind of our personality, and part of it we probably grew into over time, where we kind of fell into our roles and continue to do that today. We can bounce ideas off each other to get different perspectives on things, but we don't have the same responsibilities. He can let me do what I need to do and I can let him do what he needs to do and that's been probably the most critical thing.

**Tracey:** How did you balance that personal side to the work side? Not only were you friends in business together, you were also living together. How did you manage to separate the two to stay on track?

**Michael:** That's challenging also, you have to really be able to turn it on and off at the end of the day and that can definitely be a challenge.

There's definitely instances where things carry over and something doesn't go well during the day and it's hard to just turn that off at the end of the day. But I make a real effort to do that and just really kind of treat them as independent relationships as best as possible.

We try and find time to do things socially, especially now that we're a little older and I'm married. It was also different when we were working 120 hours a week. There really was no social aspect to what we were doing. So it was 'you work, you fall asleep, you start working again', so that was pretty easy.

Now we have a little bit different lifestyles than we did. We make a point to do something outside of work and make sure that we have that time where you don't have to think about the work aspect of it and take a fresh perspective of all that and just try and keep it as separate as you can. But I'm not going to lie and say that you can always easily just go from one mentality to another mentality, but we try the best we can. We haven't killed each other yet.

**Tracey:** That's always a good thing.

**Michael:** Yeah.

**Tracey:** So you also do a lot of outsourcing. How do you find working with outsourcing? What's the best way?

**Michael:** We use a couple of different sites primarily that help us manage the outsourcing process. One is called oDesk, which is probably my favourite one.

Basically, if you're not familiar with it, it will help you locate and source outsource providers. It gives them some standardised tests so that you can see their skill sets based on these tests across all the providers that they offer in their network.

One of the great things about it is that it monitors the outsource providers activity in a very detailed way. The provider has to be logged into their system in order to be billing their time and by logging into their system it actually takes random screen shots of their work station, it measures their typing speed and it monitors if they've stopped activity for any period of time, it cuts the billing off automatically.

So it's not to say I don't trust the people I'm working with, but especially when you're getting started with new outsource providers, especially when they're not anywhere near you and you want to always have measurable results and hold them accountable to specific tasks. To be on the safe side, the monitoring tools oDesk offer are a real benefit and essentially it's automated billing as well. They might not be doing the best job and you have to make sure that you can evaluate those results in a meaningful way, but at least you know that they're doing the work for you and not just goofing off or pretending like they're doing the work and billing you for it, which could certainly happen.

I'm sure there's plenty of people that do that, but luckily we found some people and once we really found people that we like their work, we have really long relationships with them. Most of the people that work for us now have started three, four years ago at least and continue to do great stuff for us today.

**Tracey:** Have you ever had one of those sliding door moments where you just could have taken a totally different path, but now you are really glad that you stuck to your guns and kept going with the business?

**Michael:**  In terms of stopping the business or totally changing the business, I don't think so. I think that we were dedicated to it from the beginning.

There were a couple of times at the very beginning where we thought that we might not be able to pursue it anymore if we didn't start seeing some results, but fortunately for us, we were able to become relatively successful in a pretty short period of time and then continued to build on that.

So I don't think there was ever a moment where we had a decision to make after the first several months where it was like, 'I don't know if we can do this anymore.' I'll say that we've made plenty of bad decisions over the course of the last ten years and we've made decisions that have altered maybe some of the future potential of the company, for better or worse. I look back on them as unfortunate learning experiences, but things that were probably critical to the success of our company. We've been really pretty good at managing our risk.

When it's all your money and you don't have really anything to fall back on, as I was saying before, the accountability of how much you're going to spend on something and the risk level you're willing to take can be a lot more meaningful than maybe in some other cases where you have a lot of venture capital or money kind of sitting around for you.

Whenever we go into something new, we generally are pretty good about going into something slowly and if it doesn't work we can shut it down and it's really not a lot of harm done. If it does work, we can ramp it up pretty quickly because being such a small company it allows us to be really nimble and responsive to changes. We can see an opportunity and get right into it in a really short period of time.

We definitely made plenty of mistakes where I could say, 'I handled that incorrectly', but I really think that those were important learning experiences because I didn't make those mistakes again. And I knew I had opportunities when I could have made the mistake again and remembering some of the things that I did in the past definitely enabled me to handle it in a different way.

**Tracey:** Have you had anyone doubt you and how did you handle it?

**Michael:** I mean my parents thought it was a terrible idea to get into this. I had really good grades in college and I was in a great business program. I had a lot of opportunities after leaving college where I could have gone to work for probably any one of the companies that probably went bankrupt in the last year, but I probably would have been doing all right up to that point.

I don't think my family had envisioned me working out of the basement of a townhouse when I graduated college and I don't think Nate's did either. They didn't discourage me, but they definitely didn't encourage it either. I don't think they thought it was the greatest idea.

Since then, there's certainly people that have told me that I'm making a wrong decision here or something like that. Maybe not to the point of saying our whole business is going to fail, or something like that, but plenty of people that have doubted certain decisions that we've made. I can't say that I look back on too many of them and think that somebody told me something and I really should have followed what they were saying and would have been better off. So fortunately, I don't think we've made too many bad decisions.

**Tracey:** So what's some of the cool stuff you've got to do now you're not college students in your dorm room anymore?

**Michael:** We definitely still work really hard. I mean it's always cool, especially for the parents, now seeing interviews and articles and things like that.

One of our first articles was a local technology paper and it's funny about being kind of in this dorm room or home-based business. My college apartment was so small. We had this little article done. They were coming to do it and we were real excited, but the photographer, there wasn't enough space for him to get far enough back to get a photo because I was working out of a tiny room that fit my bed and desk and that's about it. He was standing on my bed, ducking beneath the ceiling, just to get far enough back to get a shot of me from the shoulders up, at my desk.

But I guess to get back to your question, some of the cooler stuff, I mean experience wise we've gone to trade shows and things like that and they're interesting. We've gotten press. We've been able to afford a lot of things that are kind of nice things to have and we can live a much nicer lifestyle than when we just graduated college, so that's nice.

I think to me, the real thing that I feel we've gotten the most from the business is, it sounds kind of cliché, just the pride of running a successful business. I don't think that there's anything that can top that. We don't work out of an extravagant office where we get to see some great view of the city out of our window, or have a secretary or something like that. There aren't a whole lot of these great little perks that we really give ourselves, and that's by choice I think, because I can enjoy coming in knowing what I accomplish on a daily basis.

When I see our product picked up at a retail store, to me that's probably the most exciting thing and probably more exciting than sitting at a nicer desk.

For me personally, definitely those little things we do on a daily basis of watching something that you grew from nothing, become something. Whether it's the business as a whole, or each individual product we put out, that has really been the most important and rewarding thing out of the business.

**Tracey:** What do you think has been the greatest skill you've had to develop over the years?

**Michael:** One would be patience. I'm not a patient person. I can be an emotional person and I've definitely chilled out over the last while. I think that's probably one of the most important things that I've developed personality wise over the last years, is that I can get as mad as I want, but it really doesn't solve the situation. I can lash out at somebody and tell them, 'You guys really screwed us over here' or 'You're really making the wrong decision' or something like that and that still doesn't get us where I want to be.

So I definitely think patience would be something that has been a very learned trait for me. Nate had that a lot more in the first place, but for me it's something I've had to develop, and I think it's benefited our business a lot by being able to make more rational decisions and not emotional decisions about things and respond to things that way.

Other skills I needed to develop—really just basic business skills. Negotiation is something that really is a learned skill. I think it takes a lot to understand how to negotiate with people successfully and get what you want out of a deal or a situation.

Overall marketing and sales. They're also things that you really just learn over time. There's nothing better than experience for something like that.

Dealing with customer after customer, I just knew nothing about how to talk to our customers when we started, and now it's like second nature to me. It's definitely something that really takes time. Some people are natural salespeople, but you really have to become comfortable with what you're selling and that only comes with experience.

**Tracey:** So if someone came up to you and said, 'I just couldn't do what you've done' what would you say to them?

**Michael:** I think you can. I think that you have to be prepared for what it really takes to do that.

I've had a few friends that have come up to me over the years, and even some recently, looking at starting businesses and they're really not confident that they can do it. I'm not going to say that anybody can just do it under any circumstances. You really have to be prepared and take a realistic approach to what it's going to take. And that's not for everybody.

To be honest at thirty years old, married with a mortgage, is a heck of a lot different situation for me to be in, if I was going to start this today, than twenty years old living on Ramen noodles in a basement.

There's a lot of people now that say, 'Well how am I going to get started?' They're around my age or in my situation and when I say, 'You could have to collateralise your home for this if you want to get any money from the bank' or, 'You could have to put up everything in your savings'. It's something that they're not really prepared to do.

With that being said, 'Can they do it?' was your question and I think that they can. I think that if you can persevere long enough, you can probably figure out a way to become at least moderately successful at what you do.

I think a lot of it's just the perseverance. Say 'I can't give up because every day is going to be a new learning experience.' And that's really what it was for us and I could imagine that would be the case for most businesses. Most people probably don't know exactly what they're doing when they get into a new business and it's just a matter of when you're going to figure out what is the right thing to do. It could come in three weeks, it could come in three years before you really figure out, 'This is making sense.'

You might have to make all kinds of adjustments to your original plan. It might look nothing like your original concept. I mean when we started out business we thought we'd have this whole service side of our business where we're sending installers out to trade 3-D experiences in people's homes or have people who created content for people to view in 3-D. That was something that we said, it was on our website when we first launched it and I don't think anybody cared at all about it so we just dropped it. When we first started, we thought that was a great idea and it wasn't.

So you have to be willing to give up the time—it's definitely going to be something that requires a lot of time—and if you have commitments to family and things like that, again it's something that you could do, it's just not something that everybody wants to do at this point.

The financial and time aspects are really the two key factors of doing it. But I think that you really could learn at some point how to be successful. Some of the things that I've told people are just really try things on the smallest scale that you can think of, just to see if you're comfortable with getting involved in it and without giving up your day job and without putting your house or all your savings on the line.

One other thing is that you really, I think, have to be modest about it. A lot of people think that entrepreneurship is a glamorous thing, at least in my experience and in a lot of people's experiences, but it's not.

You have to be very modest about everything you do because you're not an instant success, you're not instantly generating millions and millions of dollars and you have to really swallow your pride a lot. Some people think, 'I want to start this business. So I want to go out and find this great retail location and I'm going to deck it out with all these nice things and we're going to get started, and people are going to come and start buying stuff and it's going to be successful. I'm going to be the popular guy on the block because I have all these great people coming to my great new store.' Maybe that will work, but I think a lot of times that could be a very risky approach.

Does that same person want to instead work out of the den of their house and be making phone calls all day long until they get enough customers that they then feel comfortable enough to open this big store, big office location? Some people are attracted to the glamorous side of entrepreneurship that's really not always there and you have to be realistic about that. And be comfortable with the fact that that could ultimately end up costing yourself a lot of money and hurt your chances of future success if you get ahead of yourself too much.

**Tracey:** I've always found there's a lot of hard work before the glamour comes.

**Michael:** Absolutely.

**Tracey:** The glamour's just a showing of the hard work that's actually been put in.

**Michael:** That's a great point. I mean you can see it's not glamorous around here at all. We live fairly nice lifestyles, so that's where I really get the benefit of all the work that we've put in. I can do things outside of work that are enjoyable, but ten years later we're still in a warehouse with no decorations or anything, no fancies.

**Tracey:** So if you had to start over again is there anything you'd do differently?

**Michael:** That's a good question. I would say, honestly that I'd probably say no, only because everything's just been a learning experience. This won't be the last company that I work at, or for, or start probably.

There's little things that I certainly could have made a better decision on, or maybe we would have done better had we done something else, but I don't really look back and I don't focus a lot on past decisions to be honest. That's also probably something that's cliché and a lot of people would tell you, but that's also something that when you asked about things that I've learned and one of those things is probably not to dwell on things that have already happened, because it's not moving you forward.

I'm usually comfortable with the decision I make when I make it. I feel like I've done as much research or gathered as much information in order to make as right decision as possible. I look back and some things worked out and some things didn't. But I look back and say, 'Well, I made that decision, I was comfortable with it then, so I'm going to deal with the consequences of it now, positive or negative.'

So I don't think there's anything that I wish I had done. There's maybe things I should have done differently, but not necessarily. I don't look back and say, 'All these things are bugging me that I would have done it differently under those circumstances'.

**Tracey:** So is there anything that you do on a regular basis to build that belief and that success for yourself?

**Michael:** I just focus a lot on research and gathering information. That's really what my job is. To feel like I'm qualified to make the right decision at the time for anything that comes up in the business. I don't do meditation or anything like that. That's kind of like a personal thing to build my own confidence or I just always want to feel like I'm informed about anything that relates to our business and not making an uninformed decision about anything. If I feel like I can do that, then I never lack in the confidence to move forward.

**Tracey:** Have there been any mentors or books that have really changed how you've done things or that you look back and go, 'Yeah, that was something that really helped me?'

**Michael:** Sure. I think that even in the first company I worked for when I was still in college, I don't think I could have been nearly as successful at this business had I not gotten some of that experience.

Not necessarily because it overlapped specifically with everything I do here, but I had some very smart people that I worked with and it really taught me about ways to approach situations: leadership styles, management, basically leadership-type traits; how to kind of run business in a professional way, working with other people and collaborating with other people.

It taught me things not to do, certain characteristics that people have that I probably didn't envy or didn't think would be productive for our business. That was something that was very helpful. It did give me an opportunity to kind of practice some of the skills that helped us a lot for this business. In financial planning, in even the ecommerce aspect, which I was responsible for at that company, I learned a lot of the skills that allowed me to kind of give better direction. Even though I wasn't programming everything myself, I could give better directions to the people that worked with us because I had done that before.

There are other people that I don't know personally that I could say are not mentors but positive role models. Somebody like Richard Branson is probably my number one. I think it's unbelievable how he started so many diverse companies. They're all entrepreneurial companies. He starts them with these small teams, he goes into areas that are dominated by big players like the airline industry, the music industry, and somehow finds a way to be successful—even though it might not have been related to any one of the core businesses that he's had before. He also has a very charismatic personality.

Probably the most influential book that I've ever read from a business perspective, and I've read a bunch, is Dale Carnegie's *Lifetime Plan for Success*. It is fairly well-known and is about leadership, consulting—and it's actually a very old book, but the content is just as relevant now as it was when he wrote it.

It's extremely helpful for learning how to deal with people and mainly just interact with people; how to get people to understand where you're coming from on things and how to communicate better with people. When I was reading it, it was like, these are all commonsense kind of anecdotal pieces about how to deal with this particular situation, but for some reason, it never clicked completely with me until I read it on the pages and he put it into such context that it really finally clicked.

Certain characteristics and personality traits of people just really clicked with me. And I think it really changed a lot of how I deal with people, communicate with people and I think it's helped us a lot. It's helped me learn more patience as well. That was one of the big books that helped me kind of figure out that I had to do more.

**Tracey:** So if someone was to get started in their own home-based business, or they're already in it, what would be your top tips for helping them become more successful?

**Michael:** One, the primary thing, is to really be accountable for all of the money you spend and if you're already working out of your home you've probably got a pretty good handle on that. I would say to continue to be diligent about that, even as you become successful.

I think in this recent economic downturn it's interesting to me to watch how many businesses thought that the economic climate at that time, which was going *too* well, and was so sustainable, would never change. They over expanded or started doing things that really were not consistent with how they built the initial success of their companies and they really put their whole company in jeopardy by doing that.

A lot of these businesses were doing just fine until they really took on the new attitude about how accountable they were for certain things or tried to change the decisions that had made them successful in the first place. Some of them are not here at all anymore. Starbucks is cutting way back, Mrs. Fields is gone. There's lots of these businesses that made sense, but just really over expanded. So always maintain that discipline—even as things start getting more successful for you.

You can certainly ask for help from outside places, like outsourcing is a great tool to use. It can be challenging to find somebody that really does things the way you want, preferably from the beginning, but you've kind of got to sort through that process and ultimately outsourcing can be a great tool to find people that will get things done for you at a much lower cost than bringing in a lot of staff. Especially if you're a home-based business.

Outsourcing is probably the best tool to help ramp up your business, because you obviously can't hire a tonne of people when you're working out of your house. Not having to manage the human resources aspect of this team that you have working with you, as well as just not having the physical presence, can really help you expand before you have to leave that home environment, which is a big step.

I mean taking on a lease and having to outfit an office can be a considerable expense, so it's really your biggest step. You can delay it for as long as you're comfortable with doing that, and there's no reason to jump right into it. There's office rental, office parks, conference rooms and virtual offices if you feel like your business could really benefit from a more corporate look and feel. There are these virtual offices that are great for that, which for thirty or forty or fifty dollars a month you've got a secretary answering your phone and a conference room to use if you have an important meeting that you want to be face-to-face. You don't need to jump into something that you're not comfortable with until you're ready to.

From a marketing and sales perspective, you can really benefit a lot from sticking to a grassroots type marketing. There is, especially now with the way things can travel around the internet, social networking and other things like that. These are great tools. Or if you really have a great product or a great service, it's easier than ever for the word to spread, so it can really help you get the word out, so long as you have a great service or a great product. If you don't, it's easier than ever for people to find out bad information about you. I hate it when I see a bad review on a website and it's so accessible to people. Search engines will find it and anybody can find it. So you always want to make sure you have a good product or service. But you can get it out the message to people easily, also along with sales and marketing.

We focused primarily on PR as our sales and marketing strategy when we were starting and we still do today. We don't spend a lot on proactive sales or marketing in terms of buying a lot of pages in magazines or other types of traditional media advertising.

We focus a lot on search engine marketing. We get it in front of targeted people and can control our costs and can manage our costs on a daily or minute-to-minute basis if we need to and measure those results very easily. When we're managing traffic through our website we can see everything that happens and make decisions very quickly about what campaign to increase or decrease, or any changes we need to make.

But from a strictly PR perspective, what's probably better for your customers is to get the editor of a magazine to tell them how great your product is, then it costs you the price of one product compared to taking out a full page ad for ten thousand dollars where you have to market to somebody to convince them how great your product is. We really built our success on just that, on developing relationships with the media and getting our products reviewed and mentioned by people who were not us. Their readership was much more likely to follow their suggestion than if we had taken out an ad and paid a lot of money for it.

We tried that and it can be great and I don't want to say that it's not great under any circumstances, but in my personal experience we benefited a lot more by developing relationships on the PR side, than on the advertising side. So especially as a new business, keep plugging away at the PR, the media representatives and if you can get picked up by a few it can really start a snowball effect and more people will take notice of that ball—especially if you have something unique and interesting.

**Tracey:** What's the most exciting PR that you've ever got, that you sort of jumped up and down and went, 'Oh, I can't believe we got that!'

**Michael:** There have been a couple. In terms of the biggest, we've been in some pretty sizeable magazines. *Maxim* magazine and some of the bigger men's magazines, as well as some of the local publications—you know, the smaller and more niche publications. We've been in international publications, we've been on CNBC and some of the bigger media outlets.

In terms of some of the most interesting PR, there is one thing that I did a few years ago that I thought worked out really well, which didn't necessarily generate the most sales, but it was just an interesting experience.

There was a lot of talk about 3-D being used in one of the new Nintendo systems that was coming out. It had nothing to do with us, we weren't associated in any way, it was not even going to work with our product. I had an idea to issue a press release denying the fact that we were going to be involved with that product in any way whatsoever, to shoot down all the rumours and speculation about our products being involved with this product in any way. Which was completely true, we were not involved and Nintendo probably had no idea who we even were. It had been mentioned a couple of times on the internet that maybe this company, eDimensional, is going to be involved. So I issued a whole press release how we're not doing it and it got picked up everywhere. I thought that was interesting.

By just associating our name next to the name Nintendo in all these major publications it was great PR for us. I mean it raised the profile of our company by just mentioning the two names together and there's nothing untrue about it or anything like that; it was just a way for us to feel like we could get mentions in publications and associate us with a huge brand. Like I said, just to be mentioned in the same paragraph is a great PR opportunity.

**Tracey:** Something you didn't mention in your tips was work ethic, but that's something that's really come across to me, the high amount of work ethic you have. So what is it that makes you get up every day and keep working at that intensity that you had when you were even doing the 120 hours?

**Michael:** We've definitely been able to cut back a little bit since then and I think that that's important, you can't keep that up forever. I think that was part of my nature beforehand, I was always somebody who enjoyed working and that made it a lot more manageable when we were getting started.

The thing that allows me to keep doing it is just I can set little milestones for myself and achieve them on a daily basis. I think that's really what can keep you going. You don't have to set huge goals or have this giant success to feel like you're making any progress or feel like it's worth it that you're coming in that day. I mean if you set something too big and too far off in advance, it can make it really challenging and you'll feel like you're not making any progress. When you have little projects that you can keep yourself kind of busy with, while still maintaining the overall goals of the company and making sure that you're driving towards a long term vision or goal, it becomes a lot easier to feel like you've accomplished something every day.

I don't like going home at the end of the day feeling like I wasted that day. I hate that feeling where I didn't accomplish something good then it's like, 'Well what did I do?' So I try and find at least something that I feel like I moved forward every day.

**Tracey:** I think a lot of people out there are under the misconception that it's pretty easy to get a business started. They don't realise that there is going to be a period of time where you do have to put in those hard yards to get it up off the ground and I think that's clearly evident in your story, what you and Nate did to get it going. Not a lot of people would do that, work around the clock just having some naps.

**Michael:** Right, it's hard. It just depends on what you feel like you can give at whatever point in life you're at and what other commitments you have as part of your daily life and how much money you have behind you. You can certainly hire help if you have a lot more money. It's just a choice that you want to make. Do you want to keep that for yourself or can you reinvest some of that additional profit back into the business and grow it.

If you're comfortable with what you have, the cash flow position that you're in and with whatever resources that you have available to you—manage it in a little bit more relaxed way than we did when we first started. We didn't have the option, we had no money. Finally we hired an eight or nine dollar an hour high school kid part-time and slowly built from there. But, yeah, there's really a bunch of factors and it's what you're comfortable with.

## *After the interview . . .*

Yes, I also got to meet Nate, Michael's business partner.

What was really interesting was that this wasn't their first business venture together. Over one summer when they were sixteen years old, they had a very successful car detailing business. Both have had separate businesses too, all before they started eDimensional at college. Their entrepreneurial talents started at a young age.

We also discussed how it is much easier to run a business in a partnership when the money is good.

I think Michael and Nate are great role models for showing that it doesn't matter what your circumstances are, or who you are, you can build a successful business from very modest beginnings.

In a society where it seems the majority of people are looking for the quick fix, quick service, quick road, Michael and Nate prove that diligent hard work and confidence will get you there every time.

There is no shortcut to success, but I'm sure if we asked these guys if it was worth it, they'd say yes.

Thanks Michael (and Nate) for your leading example.

For more information on Michael, check out:

www.edimensional.com

*Introducing . . .*

# Chris Malta

A man on a mission! That is how I'd describe Chris Malta. Chris has made his millions (and still does today) through the internet. His company, Worldwide Brands, is an amazing online portal to link you directly to wholesalers without a middleman.

When I caught up with Chris at beautiful Mt Shasta, in Northern California, he was on his 'Scambusters' tour. He was travelling all over the USA on a road trip to bring awareness to e-biz scammers. Passionate is an understatement when describing Chris on this topic.

I chose to interview Chris for you because I wanted to bring you a person who if you met them on the street, you'd never guess he was a multimillionaire. Using his integrity and spirit for fighting for the underdog, Harley riding Chris proves that all of us can create a business to produce significant cash flow.

## *Interview with Chris Malta . . .*

**Tracey:**  Chris, can you tell us your story please?

**Chris:**  Well the business end of it I guess goes back to when I was ten years old, believe it or not. My father worked in construction and eventually ended up buying and owning a construction company that worked in seven states, built houses in seven states.

My mother was the original, I guess you would call her today an online entrepreneur. Back then she was the party plan queen. You remember the party plan? Tupperware. They're still out there, you know. Parkland Jewelry. Whenever she got into a new party plan, she was district manager within like six months, she was really good at it.

She was doing home business when I was a little kid. I saw home business when I was a little kid. She had a shipping and packing station in our basement. I'd go downstairs and we had plastic bags on rollers. My dad built this long bench and all the stuff would come in from Tupperware or whatever in big boxes and we'd take stuff out and fill orders and fill bags and staple them with the orders and set them aside. Then she'd deliver them to her party managers and stuff.

So I saw that since I was probably four or five years old. I always knew that she loved to do that and she was really good at it. There were months that she made more money than my Dad did and he was building houses in seven states. She bought him a pool table for our house one time that he didn't want to buy because it was so expensive, on her money. He was always amazed at how well she could do at home business when he was out there and he had eighty people working for him and he had all these construction crews in different states and still sometimes she made more money than he did.

When I was ten, I wanted to make some extra money for Christmas to buy presents for the family, so I was out shovelling driveways freezing myself to death. The winter up near Lake Ontario in New York gets very cold. She said, 'Let me show you how the big people do it.'

She took me down to a wholesale warehouse where she used to get her prizes for her parties and introduced me to Beansy Altman who was a really nice older guy that had a big wholesale place down in Rochester, New York. She helped me buy some Christmas candles and little plastic wreaths that went around little plates.

I took those and went around the neighbourhood and sold them to all the ladies in the neighbourhood and made money doing that. Ever since then, every holiday that came up, I'd get more seasonal stuff from Beansy's and go out and sell it to the neighbourhood and make money.

Ever since then, I just couldn't help it, I had to work for myself. Every job I've ever had, I could never stand it. I went as far as I did through my education, eventually to being systems engineer and working for Kodak's world headquarters, I still couldn't stand it because it had to be for myself.

All those years I always had a side business, from the time I was old enough to file a DBA, a legal business, I always had a business going on the side doing something. At one point my mother and I had a business: we noticed that my uncle who was in a nursing home, couldn't fasten his own clothing very well anymore. We kind of looked into it and we found that we could replace the buttons and the zippers and the stuff with Velcro closures. We went out and started a company called 'Golden Age Apparel,' and we hired a couple of people and bought wholesale clothing out of local New York and put together a book called a catalogue and went to nursing homes and places like that and we sold that stuff. I was probably nineteen when we were doing that. I had a video production business for a while. Just all kinds of businesses.

I first went online in 1993 back when we had twenty-eight hundred bug modems and just getting online was an adventure in itself, you know? But we had newsgroups back then. There were the newsgroups, I was selling at ten or fifteen bucks I think; information on working with Microsoft computers because I was a systems engineer and I knew a lot of stuff other people didn't. I'd put together little electronic booklets and sell those to the newsgroups.

I came around to online stores in 1997 or 1998 I think it was, and started that. My first store was a disaster because I tried to build a department store, everything to everybody, and you can't do that, it's too complicated. Even today, even more so, they don't work well because you have to be very focused on a niche market. But even back then when Yahoo! started brand new and there weren't really store platforms out there, when you worked with a Yahoo! store your source of traffic was Yahoo! shopping. If you owned a Yahoo! store, you were part of Yahoo! shopping and they went out and did the TV and radio ads and newspaper ads that brought everybody into Yahoo! shopping. Then the traffic split up from there.

So it wasn't a big search engine SEO thing like it is now. It's you have to be part of this shopping platform, they'll do the advertising and if you happen to sell what people want, then you can sell. The Yahoo! store didn't do well except for one product and that was electronic dart boards and for some reason I was selling those. The dart shop itself I opened and I closed the department store. I said, 'I need to follow the money, because you're the product that's selling, the rest of them aren't.'

I opened a shop that focused on just darts and dart boards and puzzle boards and a couple of other games. When I had that running for a little while I put up a page of information on that site that talked about all the different rules and all the different games you could play with those boards, they're all made by the same company.

That page became the most popular page on the site because people would refer to it over and over again. They're having a couple of beers at the pub right, and they're playing darts and somebody might say 'You can't do that, let's go check the rules'. So they'd come to my page and check the rules. On that page of rules was always, 'Hey, are you ready for a new set of flights? Check out this new board we just got in' and that would bring them into the products.

That sold so well that during that time, I was getting to know my manufacturer very well, which you need to do if you're in business. You can't just order from a wholesaler and never talk to them. You have to know your manufacturer's rep because they're the people who can help you as you move through your business.

So I spent time getting to know my manufacturer's rep and was talking to her one day and she mentioned the fact that the company was getting out of drop-shipping altogether because it was too timely and costly. I said, 'Would you let me take it over?' And she said, 'Well let's talk about it.' And she did.

I was living in Florida at the time, I had a friend in New York who had a warehouse he wasn't doing anything with and I called him. I flew up there and they agreed to do it and he agreed to partner with me on the business. We opened Empire Global Wholesale Distribution. That was in the late 1990s, early 2000s, I think.

What we did was we filled up the warehouse with darts and dart boards and we became the internet distributors for internet sellers. That worked pretty well for a while. He was unfortunately unable to spend the time that required for him to keep up their end of the business so we ended up getting rid of that company. But I now became the exclusive wholesale distributor of this whole line of dart boards just from one little Yahoo! store. It was amazing—it was only in the course of maybe a year and a half.

I'm going to step back for a minute because getting into the whole online store, the department store itself, was where all of my brands came from—this whole directory company came from.

At first, I was trying really hard looking online trying to find wholesale suppliers for all of the different things I wanted to sell online, too many different things it turned out, but I spent a lot of time looking for wholesalers online and finding middlemen.

I would get somebody who would say, 'We're a wholesaler of this and this and this.' Well great, set up an account with them, wait for it to mature, get the price list, find out that they're really not wholesale, they're someone pretending to be a wholesaler. They've got a wholesale account with a real distributor. They turn around and say, 'We are the wholesaler' and they just jack the profit up, sending orders around to the real people.

That's what most of it is, probably 98 percent of everything you see when you go into Google or any search engine and look up *wholesale, wholesale distributor*, those kind of things, they are just middlemen. The bad guys know that's the space to hang in to cheat you and they do. Even back then, twelve years ago, eleven years ago, they knew that.

I couldn't find real wholesalers online. Then I realised I'd always known where to find real wholesalers, you go to the manufacturer. I mean my mother taught me that years ago. So I started finding what I wanted to sell, calling the manufacturers of those products and saying, 'Who are your wholesalers?' Because they make the stuff, they know who wholesales it, right? It was really easy to get to the wholesalers. I took the time because the research takes time, and then finding a company that actually wants to sell to online sellers was tough because they don't like their products being devalued in the market place. A lot of manufacturers and wholesalers feel that online sellers are inexperienced and the only thing they know how to do is cut price, cut price, cut price, cut price, so what that does is devalue the products in the market place.

These people that make all of these things don't want their products selling cut rate on eBay, having their retails stores screaming at them saying 'What are you doing? I'm not buying any more of your stuff because we can't sell it at those prices, we have lights to pay for.'

I checked out a few wholesalers and I had written an article that I kind of put out there, just something to ease things along a lot of the time. *Webpro News* picked it up and ran it and it was about that very problem, about how to find real wholesalers and the fact that you can't because there's so much garbage out there. They ran the article and they had a really good response. They came back and asked me for a follow-up, describing exactly how I do it. So I did, I wrote a follow-up.

I described how to talk to manufacturers and find wholesalers. They included my email address and I got an avalanche of emails really wanting those sources I found. I'd just spent three months chalking up those sources, I'm not just going to give them away.

So I think for like $14.95 or something like that I put up a little list of a dozen wholesalers. Here, if you really want them and I'll just keep researching more and keep adding to the list. That's where it got started.

The first couple of years I was manually building that webpage. I worked more and more and more on the research. I had the dart shop running and was working on a couple of online stores, but I was a real information salesman, which I'd started in 1993, when I found a niche. I started doing the research and building the list.

I had to do it in those days by hand. Every time I found a new distributor I had to manually update the web pages and re-alphabetise everything. I was putting in the product types and everything and I had to go in and actually physically edit the web page and re-alphabetise all the listings.

I did that for maybe a year and a half, two years, the beginning of all my brands. Then we finally built everything into the main page. That's kind of where that started and that was a need that I had and I found a solution to it. I wrote about it and everybody wanted the solution, so I was able to provide the solution.

Now today we have, I don't even remember how many employees we have, it's a multimillion dollar company. We're part of eBay and Amazon and UPS and all these big companies. In the early days I had to go try to talk to them about promotional things and they didn't want to talk to us. These days now I have executives from all these big companies actually fly out and see us, which is great. It's back and forth, we go out and see them, except on this trip we'll be going through San Jose and I'll be spending some time with a couple of US people. But they'll come out and actually see us now and once you get on their radar it's very nice.

**Tracey:** Can you describe what Worldwide Brands does now?

**Chris:**  Okay, so it's a directory of real, qualified wholesalers, who would all sell to online retailers without question. We go through this twenty-one, twenty-two point check list with our researchers. They verify with the Chamber of Commerce that the company is real. The company signs an electronic agreement with us stating that they'll follow our policies and work with our customers.

Nobody else does, we are the only company that goes to the time and trouble to actually do that. Over the years now we've qualified more than eight thousand wholesalers that represent over ten million products to sell online.

In our directory you don't just find a name of a business you find the name of the person to talk to at the business, their phone number, their email address, their shipping methods, what kinds of payments they accept, the listings of their product types and all the different things they sell, samplings of their products, the whole thing.

We put it all together so that you can instantly start working with these people. When you call them and say I found you on Worldwide Brands, they know who we are, so it's okay. They can qualify for a pre-account, we'll set you up and get you on. The other side of it is the research, the market research.

About maybe five years ago we actually had five different products for sale at our company. We had a drop ship directory, a light bulb wholesale directory which is slightly larger quantity; a bolt directory liquidation, then the market research tool that we developed. There's like five different products. Then the marketing got confused, so we took about six months and rolled those all into one and that's what Worldwide Brands is now.  It's the search engine that helps you do your market research and figure out what to sell.  It's the wholesalers who provide the products for you to sell, then it's the market research tool to tell you how well things are selling online now. It's a whole nineteen-chapter education: the video education that we did that teaches you how to work with wholesalers, how to work in retail, how to figure out some of your accounting issues, other things like that that are also around wholesale and products.

**Tracey:**  What do you think has been the skill that's been the best for you to learn over these years? What have you had to really develop?

**Chris:** I didn't really develop—but I learned a little bit of everything. Because if you don't know how everything in your business works, even if you outsource—and I mean, I read a blog post about this recently—even if you outsource and farm out certain parts of your business, if you don't know how they work first, then you can't see the big picture.

I have a few employees in my company, my partner, my business partner and I have employees who do a lot of different things. They know their jobs really well and they do them really well. They know a little bit about their co-workers jobs but I, and my partner Rob to a certain extent, know just about everything.

We know how to do just about everything and we can look at everyone and say, 'Okay, well, one person said here he did this and another person says that.' I can look at it and say, 'No, this is how this really works so this is how you two are going to make it and do it.'

I find myself doing everything from sometimes quoting, web pages to having conversations to create new business partnerships. It's the whole range. So the most important thing that I had to learn was how to know enough about everything without getting overwhelmed about all things.

I like to be hands on and I like to know what I'm doing. I spent a lot of time working with AS Construction Company, hammer, nails, tools; he's an electrician, plumber, carpenter, he's the whole thing. I like to know how everything works and how to do everything. But there's just so many people now who are willing to pay somebody else to do stuff for their business without understanding how it works first, I think that's a mistake.

I've had one woman come through a workshop recently who all she wanted to know was who she could pay to do everything? She said, 'Okay, I want to write a blog, who can I pay to write a blog? Who can I pay to write articles for me? Who can I pay to build my web site? Who can I pay to do my process? Who can I pay to do my record research?' That's all she wanted to know. I said, 'Do you want to make money or spend money? I don't understand, I'm confused here. What is your goal?' She was going to spend a lot more than she was ever going to make.

I used to manage our affiliate program a long, long, long time ago. Now Kelly Darwin does a fantastic job of that. I don't even have to look at it anymore, she's really good. What I did was the early stuff. It's been developed by her and other people in the business much more now. I know how it works, I know what the theory is and I know if I need to get in there and do something I can, but I'm much better off to let them do it.

Same thing with marketing and all those kinds of things that we do. You have to be able to, as you bring people into your business, hand off pieces and let go of those pieces. That's the hardest part, to actually let go of things and say, 'Okay, it's yours now. Oh, wait a minute, no, no, okay it's yours, go ahead.' That's the hardest thing to do when you started by yourself and built it.

**Tracey:** In those early days when it was more you by yourself, was there ever a time that you doubted what you were doing, or if you could actually make it go all the way?

**Chris:** No, I don't think there ever was and I still don't think there is. I think that's probably the result of my mother always telling me, 'You're smart, whatever you try to do you can be successful' and she was right.

It's always in the back of mind that I don't have to worry about it, as long as I put in the time and the work and learn, think about what I'm doing. I've never really worried that will it be successful or not. If I think it's a good idea, she gave the confidence that I trust that it's a good idea.

I know a lot of people don't have that. I mean a lot of people unfortunately have a lot of people around them who say, 'You're out of your mind. You're doing a what? What's an online business?' Their friends, their families will tell them.

I had some people around me too that told me that. I was making a six figure income as a systems engineer and starting an online business and people are saying 'What are you talking about? Don't miss your time. Don't blow your job'. But people need to overcome that if they can get some support system going with their family or friends or whatever, at least try to help them understand. They need that.

**Tracey:**  You were mentored by your parents. They obviously had a huge impact and it's amazing how many people talk about that their parents had a huge impact. How does it feel now to actually go and mentor other people and help them?

**Chris:**  I think when I know that their light bulb has clicked on, when I'm talking to someone and you see, 'Ah, now I get it. That's what they mean when they say that? Okay, well now I get that'. That's great, right there.

You talk to them and you kind of wait for that to happen. As you're talking, you're going down different roads, different subjects. Everyone's experience in business is going to be different, nobody can take a cut-and-dried program step one through ten or twenty, do all those steps and be successful. You can't, everyone has different knowledge, different backgrounds, different motivations, different skill sets, different level of intelligence, different everything, right? Everything has to kind of be designed around that individual person.

I talk to different people in different ways. There's some people that you can tell, ten minutes into a conversation, you can tell they need a kick in the pants. Then there are some people who just need to be spoken to calmly, 'Okay, just come around and reason this out with me now.' Other people need to be told, 'Look, if you don't drop this now and turn around and do it the other way, you might as well just mail somebody the money and forget about it—give it to somebody.' But in every case, no matter how you're working with people, you almost always get to that point where they get it all of a sudden.

That's really a reward, that's really cool because you know that at least you got that through to them and now they're not going to make those mistakes. Then we'll go onto the next subject and get them to have another moment, another epiphany along the way. The more of those you can get them to have and the more you can get them working with other people.

That's another thing that I do that's really, really important, is I have a private forum where people who go through my workshops and people who just come in from the outside and pay for it, work together.

It's only a few hundred people—it just started last year. But the people in there work together so well because it is a paid, private forum. It's not a place where you can just jump in and out, people just running in and out and paying other people and doing stupid things that they do in forums. Because they're paying for it they're much more serious. That whole support system and all those people having those little epiphanies all the time and communicating with each other. When they do, it's huge. It's a small group of people but it's a huge thing to see happening.

**Tracey:** I often say that sometimes being in small business, especially a home-based business, it can be like the loneliest place in the world and so sometimes it's really nice to have those other people who are understanding and they know where you're at and they're positive about helping.

**Chris:** Exactly, because their families aren't, well, a lot of them say their families aren't supporting them. The wives are telling them they're crazy, the husbands are telling them they're nuts, the kids are saying, 'I want a new pair of shoes.' Having those people that are going through the same issues, at the same time is a big, big thing for them.

**Tracey:** If someone was going to get started in what a lot of people see as the best home-based business—an online business—what things should they get started with first and what's the best way if they don't have a lot of experience in an online business?

**Chris:** If they don't have a lot of experience or even if they think they do, don't believe anything that tells them it's easy.

That's the first thing I always tell people when they come to me, to a workshop, they blog, they write, or they call, whatever, they do the email and they say, 'What do I do first?' First thing is take off the rose-coloured glasses because it's not easy.

It's going to take work, time and some money. It doesn't have to take a lot of money, but you have to research a little bit. You have to understand that people who tell you it's easy are lying to you. After that, beyond the whole scam-busting things (that's my favourite soapbox, I'll sit on that all day) it's basically four things. You get legal, you find a product to sell, find a platform to sell on and work on your market. Within those four things are a tremendous amount of subsections that you need to work on.

I have a friend in New Mexico, he's a good example. For years he would call me every once in a while and say, 'Hey, I really want to get started online, what do I do?' And I told him, 'Kevin, just take something out of your house and sell it on eBay. Just get the experience one time of making a sale, completing a sale with a customer.' He didn't do it and he did have a lot of things going on and he was busy with this and that and working a couple of jobs. He called me again, 'I want to get started online', Kevin says. Again, find something and sell it on eBay.

Finally he did. He has a big collection of vintage Hot Wheels cars, a lot of them still in their original packets. So he just took one of those and went out and did a little research and sold it online. Now he's going back and forth emailing all the time. He just had to break the ice and get the experience. But make sure that you don't let anybody make promises that they're going to do anything for you or make it easy for you. You have to do the work and the research.

**Tracey:** So if you could share some of those scamming experiences, because I think it helps, the more that we can get that story out that there are these people out there. I think that's in any business, even in retail businesses, store fronts. There's always going to be people who are trying to do the wrong thing, take advantage of people.

**Chris:** Well, really you just said it, it's the snake oil salesman. They're in all businesses, they always have been and the internet's no different.

What a lot of people don't understand is that the internet is not a magic flat box that you just have to find the right person to sell you the gold key and everything's going to work. It's nothing different; it's retail sales. It's retail sales just like retail sales has always been, from a trading post in the Arabian desert, to Montgomery Ward, to a catalogue from the late 1900s, to Macy's today, to the internet. It's just retail sales. It's, 'I've got a product here, do you want to buy it? I'll tell you about it. Give me your money and you can have it.' That's all it is.

Everybody puts up so much hype about all these programs and tools and all this other stuff that you need. Yeah, it's a different set of tools than having a physical retail store, because in a retail store you have shelves and you have a cash register and you have a door and a sign; all that stuff, a couple of people working in there, some decor, maybe some boring music or something. In an online store it's a different set of tools, but it's still retail.

If you think about a retail store, if you're going to open one would you go out and look for somebody to do it for you? Or would you go rent the space and put up the shelves and order the products and sell the stock? You'd go do it yourself. Don't go set up in the mall and, 'I think I'd go find somebody who can go open the shoe store for me while I sit at home.' It's just a no brainer, you'd do the work yourself.

So anybody who tells you that it's easy or anyone who promises you a certain amount of money, anyone who tells you that this is an easy business, anyone who tells you that they're going to do it for you, anyone that tells you they have all this built in traffic that's going to make you money, anyone that promises you certain amounts of money by the month or by the year, is flat out lying to you. It's not true, none of it.

It's all part of a very, very large network of affiliate marketers and telesales people. A great deal of it is based in Utah. Some of it claims to be in Arizona, California, New York, things like that, but what they do is largely disguise who they are, they disguise their names, they disguise their servers where they keep their IP addresses. They hide their information on the Internet. You can't look at their domain name because it's got like Domains by Proxy, for example, who'll hide that for a few bucks.

So you can't find out who they really are. But most of them are based in Utah and that has a lot to do with the fact that a lot of the telemarketing industry is based in Utah. That's where the sales floors are, so that's where these companies go to take advantage of that telemarketing infrastructure. They put out what are called lead generators which are cheap programs that seem to do what the good stuff does.

In the first four to five years I used to manage and handle all the issues of copycats and deal with them, copyright and that stuff. When we got a bigger wholesale base it happens all the time. I still have on my computer at home, ninety separate folders of different companies and people who stole our information in the first four or five years and tried to resell it. Since then, there's been a lot more. In the last five years, I haven't managed that stuff.

We catch people. Let me see, there's one company, I won't even mention who they are because we've been in legal issues with them, but they took our information and started copying it verbatim. And again, this is what the scammers do, they find other stuff and they take bits and pieces of things they think are legitimate. They only take a little bit, because they don't want to get caught. Then they jam it altogether and it really isn't anything cohesive, it's just a jumbled together mess of a little bit of information from here and there and there—whatever they could steal without being caught. That's what they sell you. And it's useless, but they tell you it's worth tens of thousands of dollars.

There's one company, just one of many who do the same thing, they were stupid enough to copy our information verbatim. You know 'Wholesale Directory' in the comments fields? Their website, in their directory, it still said, 'Tell your wholesaler you found us through Worldwide Brands.' They didn't even look. In fact we found that they outsourced it to somebody in India to copy our stuff to try to keep themselves distant from the actual fact.

They did this. We found out about it, but they thought they were safe because they were out of the US because my business partner is a movie producer, he has entertainment industry attorneys and we use those same attorneys for our business getting our lawful property. They have partner firms all over the world.

So these guys found that out pretty quickly and we caught them and fired off some legal letters and they suddenly wrote back and they started to offer us this money not to prosecute. But they said there's one condition, 'You can't ever talk about us online, you can never say anything about us online.' We said, 'Forget it, I don't want your money. Take the stuff down. I'm going to hold this over your head. If I ever see you doing this again I'm going to prosecute.' There's the solution to that because too many of them just started cheating people in all directions.

These companies work with very, very high pressure salespeople. They will give you an offer on TV, the late night infomercials, they'd sell you an easy internet business, easy to set up, you'll make all kinds of money. The real estate programs too, all those things, all those infomercials, they all lead to the same thing. They sell you something small and that turns into something bigger and bigger and bigger until you're caught up in this web so much that you can't get out and you feel your only way to make your money back is to keep paying them more money to buy the next level.

So they keep building you up level to level to level, telling you that you have to buy the current stuff to make the original stuff work. You'll end up with having spent ten, fifteen, twenty, thirty, forty thousand dollars.

I know a woman in South Carolina who went through this mess. She's seventy-two years old, she's a widow and she's on social security and they took her as far as getting her to refinance her house and they got her for ninety thousand dollars.

They took her through all the online garbage they were doing, then they threw her over into the real estate side and took her through all that junk they were selling. And ninety grand later she's losing her house and she's got nowhere to go. This happens on a daily basis, every single day.

There is a company, actually a couple of companies, that go around and have these big hotel seminars where they invite you to free meetings at a hotel all day long and they'll buy you lunch and they want to talk to you about e-commerce business, right?

I've been to these things that at least one of these companies has invited me to. Their executive invited me so I can go up and they want me to promote them. So I go. The last one I went to I sat in the back of the room with a notepad and instead of listening to all the hype, I just totaled up all the dollar figures I heard. It was over six hours. They would bring some innocent guy from the local news station, the sportscaster from the local news station to come up and be the face guy, jump around, warm up the crowd, make everybody laugh, you know? Then the company executive comes up and says, 'With this $200 you can have this wonderful tool that's going to make you all kinds of money.'

The face guy comes back and jumps around some more and distracts the crowd from the original offer. And then the next guy from the business comes up and says, 'For just $999 you can make $10,000 a month.' Then he goes away, they bring up the clown again, distract them from that offer, then the next guy comes up and makes another offer. By the time they were done I had totaled a whole $9,000 on my notepad. I was tracking what they were saying and the price. At the end of the meeting they had these people so hyped up that they were lining up to give them their credit cards.

The guy took me aside, this executive took me aside and said 'Today we're going to sell half the people in this room.' There were two hundred people there. And he said, 'In the next two weeks we'll get 25 percent more', half of the rest of them. And they offered me, I think it was either a $2,000, or $2,500 commission, for everybody I sent to them who bought.

Needless to say I never did it because I know what they were doing to those people. They give them websites that are garbage, their templates are horrible, they can't be changed. If you want to make any changes to the site you have to pay them to reprogram them. The promises they make are worthless.

They promise coaching, but what they really do is they give you maybe thirty minutes a week, four times over the course of a period of months. Some of them will do it half an hour to an hour a week for a couple of months. But during the coaching sessions, say your first coaching session you're supposed to get from lesson one to lesson four, that's your homework for the next one. If you only got to lesson two and you don't understand something in your next session you start from lesson five. They will not take you back to lesson two and explain what you're missing.

What they are, these people who are these coaches, they're paid eight to twelve dollars an hour and I know this from industry insiders who I've talked to. They're paid eight to twelve dollars an hour, they work from home and they're reading a script. They're not business people who are coaching people to help them understand business. They're just people who answer ads in the newspaper who have done some kind of phone work before and they just give these people a script and they say, 'Here, make these phone calls and read this stuff to them' and that's it. That's $15,000, $20,000 worth of coaching.

**Tracey:** I didn't think you were going to say $15,000 to $20,000.

**Chris:** Yeah. So that's what's going wrong with this business right now. Too many people think that it's easy. And even though there's a recession in the US and around the world at this point, which is, I'm sure, going to continue for a few more years, people are more and more desperate.

So even sometimes when they're afraid that what they're buying isn't going to work, they grasp at it anyway because it's the only thing they can think of. The sales people are playing on that. If you don't do this you could lose your house, or what if your job disappears tomorrow? They're very, very top, hard core, nasty sales people and they belittle you on the phone, they'll call you names, they'll make you feel stupid if you don't buy these things. That's just the high pressure method they use.

The biggest thing to watch out for is if they ask you to sign a contract. Don't ever, ever sign a contract either online or on a piece of paper. They all want that because they all know very shortly you're going to be coming back for a refund and they want that signature as in that contract somewhere it's going to say that you can't have a refund. Even if they promised it to you with an email or on the website or somewhere else, you can't have a refund, it's in the contract and that's how they get to keep your money. Then in the contract also there'll be wording, in most cases, that says that you can't say anything about them anywhere online or anywhere else. You can't speak poorly of them, you can't tell people your experiences with them. They've got this all locked up.

**Tracey:** That should raise some flags straight away, 'You're not allowed to say anything about us.'

**Chris:** A lot of those people don't read the contracts. They're long and they're very fine print and they're complicated and in that language it's built-in. All these things are built-in, but people never read them and even if they do read them they don't get most of those things that are happening.

**Tracey:** If someone came up to you and said, 'I just couldn't do what you've done, I couldn't turn myself from starting with next to nothing to fifteen million dollars and a business that is turning over multimillions.' What would you say to them?

**Chris:** I'd say, 'Why not? What do you think is wrong with you that you couldn't do something like that?'
     I think most of the time people get in their own way, not believing that they could do something like that. I always wanted to be self-sufficient when I was building businesses and I've always had my own businesses—for years. But it's not getting to a certain point, making a certain amount of money; it's doing what you love to do.

If you're an entrepreneur, you can't help it. You just can't, if you don't like working for other people. If you don't deal with authority well, then you're probably an entrepreneur and you'd better let that out because it will bother you the rest of your life if you don't. What I would say is don't listen to them, do it. Because it's something in your own head that's stopping you, it's not something from outside. Entrepreneurial companies built most of the world. People started small and grew.

**Tracey:** Have you got any other tips for anyone who's thinking about getting into home-based business? What would be your tips from your business experience for them?

**Chris:** I probably have a lot that I'll think of after we finish talking. Since you're getting into business, it's just *common sense*—it is such a great equaliser. It's something that so few people use. They let it fly right out the window as soon as promises of dollar signs come at them. But common sense is everything.

I've talked to people who have MBAs, I've talked to people who started from nothing, I've talked to everybody in between and you can't go by the book all the time. There's a difference between book learning and street knowledge and common sense kind of brings those two together.

It's good to have the education, but if it doesn't sound right to you, it's probably not right. I wish I could give you a list of them, of tips for starting a business, but it's really just you have to find something that people are looking for but aren't getting. It doesn't have to be something big, it can be something very simple and very small. I know people who are making money selling little glass beads for embroidery, they're making tonnes of money and they're just selling glass beads. We thought that one up, two hundred years ago, the British came over here and traded beads too. But no, you can still do that, it doesn't have to be flashy, you don't have to sell flashy products.

So many people want to get into electronics online because it's cool. They can go tell their people, their friends, yeah, they sell MP3 players, the latest games and all that stuff. That is a miserable market, there's no profit in it. People sit back quietly and sell toasters and shoes all day long and make fortunes. It's not cool, but it makes money. So you don't have to do something amazing, you don't have to invent a new mouse trap, you just have to understand retail, get into the business and just sell what people are looking for. That's all there is to it.

**Tracey:**  Where did you start your scam-busting tour?

**Chris:**  Started in New York. It happened when I was up in Syracuse, just on a trip up to Syracuse and I got that email from the woman I told you about who lost so much money and that was kind of the straw that broke the camel's back. I said, 'That's enough, I'm tired of this.' We just decided right then and there, we're going to leave from there—I live in Orlando—we're going to leave from Syracuse, New York and just start travelling and try to do something. The point of this whole trip is to raise some kind of awareness.

On my website, you haven't seen the real intent of the website yet. What it's been, is kind of a social thing, here's what we're doing, follow the videos, have some fun, enjoy this trip and we're going to try to tell you some things and educate you along the way.

But what's really going to come out of this is some detailed information on how these companies work from the inside. Where they are, really how to avoid them. Again, I want to get this in front of someone who can put it on a national news broadcast, because I think if enough people hear about it, or if the higher end news media pay attention, people can avoid being scammed.

You can go on the national news channel in the mornings and watch a story being broadcast to millions of people about how happy someone is because she lost thirty pounds. Well, what about the woman who is unhappy because she lost thirty thousand dollars? Let's talk about that instead of all this diet crap. There's got to be room in the news media for real stories and not just fluff.

I think that soon we will get more of this information in a more cohesive format. I'm going to start emailing some of the bigger news media, some of the bigger talk shows, just over and over again, every week hit them over and over and over with the story. Say, 'Hey, why aren't you paying attention to this'?

Hopefully that will be the result of this trip. We've been through New York, Pennsylvania, Ohio, Indiana, Illinois, Michigan, Minnesota, Montana, North Dakota, Washington, Oregon and now in California. So we're going down the California coast to LA and then back across the country, zigzagging through North and South Dakota and most of the major cities we missed.

So we've been going a little over three months and it could take a lot longer, but I can work from here. Mobile broadband and a laptop computer with a cell phone. I can work from anywhere. Got video editing capability with us, got a video camera, got Adobe CS3 editing software and that's all I need. A connection to YouTube and we're good to go.

Also when the personal workshops are online, a lot of times I'll be working with five people in a workshop all day long—and sometimes I tell them, sometimes I won't, just whether it comes up or not—that I'll be in a tent. Sitting in a tent in the woods running these online workshops with people. Most of the time, I just tell people that because they love to hear it. 'Oh, that's cool' because they want to do that someday.

As far as business, Worldwide Brands is always changing, it's always growing. We have recently been built in to the eBay website.

Ebay recently took, I think it's about seven companies in the world, and built their functionality and products right into the eBay website and we just had this launch about two weeks ago. We've been working on it for six months or so. The people in my office have done a fantastic job putting all that together. So now right inside of eBay Selling Manager you can actually buy the Worldwide Brands product and use it inside the eBay website. We think that's going to do big things for our company.

I've got a lot of people who run that business very well. So me and my partner are not stepped out of the company, but we're one foot here and one foot still in business. We're both running the company, but it's going so well we don't have to spend all the time there. We both love developing new things and that's what we'll keep doing.

## After the interview . . .

Chris is not only passionate about what he does and stands for, but he also has a good grasp on basic business and makes it easy to understand. Sure, online business is a great avenue and it's much more economical to get started than a traditional business, but the business principles are the same. You still have to have something to sell and you still find a market that wants to buy it.

Another thing I noticed was how much of Chris' success was linked to the core values his parents taught him. If you are a parent, I hope you noticed that too.

Chris and I chatted for some time after the interview about how people don't come out and talk about being scammed by the 'snake oil salesman.' Often times, it is because they are embarrassed. 'How could I have been so stupid?' The thing to remember is, that if by any chance this has happened to you, know you are not stupid. These people are well-trained to scam you.

Chris is a Harley riding giant (he is really tall and I'm only five foot two) who is a multimillionaire. He genuinely wants to help people. He will certainly tell you like it is, but it comes from a good place of wanting to help you.

Well done Chris and keep fighting for the underdog.

For more information on Chris, check out:

www.chrismalta.com
www.worldwidebrands.com

# In Conclusion...

Everyone has wisdom to share and everyone has wisdom to gain. If your mind and heart are open, learning, growing and helping others do the same is easy.

The life of a home-based business owner can be the most rewarding and the most frustrating experience all at the same time. How you react and respond is what will set you apart from the crowd.

Passion was a word used a lot by our eight mentors throughout their interviews and something they all demonstrated in their business and in their personal life. How passionate are you? Which of the eight entrepreneurs resonated most with you and why? Take time to think about it. Really, take the time. Don't say you will later, do it now. Take the time to reflect on their stories and the wisdom that has been shared with you. What are you going to do with that wisdom? What actions are you going to take? Who will you share it with?

My aim was to bring you inspiration, from real life stories and real people, and to encourage you to go after your dreams. My aim was to bring you courage to step out and create your success in whatever endeavour you choose to pursue.

Through this journey, I have discovered my own passion and the need for getting out and living my life. I am now asking myself the question, 'How do I want to live?' instead of, 'What do I want to do for a living?'

As a home-based business owner it is very easy to 'hide' from the world, but what I discovered from these interviews is that you need to get out in the world and discover the opportunities to help you move forward, as well as helping those around you do the same. As the world is changing, a home-based business is a great place to be. If you dream of making your millions in your PJ's, then now is the time to act. Maybe start part-time and build up your business. Think logically, but work and keep going. Persistence is the key.

When times are tough, and trust me, we all have tough times, come back to this book and reread the words of wisdom from your favourite entrepreneur. Surround yourself with people who believe in you. Find a great mentor, but most importantly believe in yourself and allow your passion to flow.

I wish you all the best in your business or your future business if you haven't yet started your journey. Please come visit me at my website **www.TheArtOfHomeBasedBusiness.com** where you will find a free e-book to help you choose the right home-based business for you, free videos, my blog, my online course and more.

I look forward to meeting you again as my journey, and yours, continues.

Do your best,

*Tracy*

To access your **FREE** videos of these interviews, please go to:

**www.TheArtOfHomeBasedBusiness.com/interviews**
(Access Code:  pjmillions)

# Would you like to get started in your own home-based business?

# Would you like to take your home business to the next level?

## Come visit us today at:
## www.TheArtOfHomeBasedBusiness.com

- **<u>FREE</u> e-book** on 'Which Home-Based Business?' The guide to help you choose the home-based business that is best for you.
- The Art of Home Based Business **Online Course** is a 12 month course where Tracey will help you learn the basics of business including how to market your business, sell your services & products, set goals, manage your time and make profit. More than just the basics and theory, also included is a step-by-step business plan to get your business off on the right foot whether you are new to business or just need to kick your business to the next level.
- Tracey regularly **blogs** on topics to add value to the home-based business owner plus check out her **<u>FREE</u> e-magazine**.
- **<u>FREE</u> videos** with hints and tips to help you further in your business.

## www.TheArtOfHomeBasedBusiness.com

Check out Tracey's blog, <u>FREE</u> webinar & download your <u>FREE</u> e-book (Which Home-Based Business?)

**www.TheArtOfHomeBasedBusiness.com**

www.ingramcontent.com/pod-product-compliance
Lightning Source LLC
Chambersburg PA
CBHW071421170526
45165CB00001B/351